The evaluation of literacy programmes

The evaluation of literacy programmes

A practical guide

Roger Couvert

unesco

Published in 1979 by the United Nations
Educational, Scientific and Cultural
Organization,
7 Place de Fontenoy, 75700 Paris
Printed by Imprimeries réunies de Chambéry

ISBN 92-3-101580-X

French edition: 92-3-201580-3
Spanish edition: 92-3-301580-7

© Unesco 1979
Printed in France

Preface

The aim of this work is to place on a scientific footing both the evaluation of literacy action at the national level and the research which underlies this evaluation.

Designed to fill, at least in part, an existing gap, this guide is addressed not only to specialists and practitioners, but more generally to all those interested in the evaluation of literacy work with adults. It constitutes an initial contribution, which will doubtless require completion by further studies, to the often complex methodology needed for the objective measurement of the results of functional literacy programmes.

The author of this *Practical Guide*, Roger Couvert, seeks to share with the reader his own experience gained during the field implementation and the final evaluation of the Experimental World Literacy Programme. A French specialist from the Office de l'Orientation Scolaire at Grenoble, Couvert has worked as a Unesco expert in a variety of countries, in particular the United Republic of Cameroon, Haiti, the Lao People's Democratic Republic and Madagascar. He has written a number of studies and articles dealing, *inter alia*, with the first three countries and covering, respectively, the subjects of educational guidance, literacy training programmes and functional literacy work. Other publications have included a discussion of the transition from school to working life and a practical guide for evaluating literacy programmes.

The text has also been enriched by comments, observations and suggestions from other specialists. Bearing particularly in mind the great variety of situations which affect literacy training, much remains to be done before all the requirements of the experts are satisfied; and the elaboration of a methodology of evaluation will depend in a certain measure on the criticisms and proposals which specialists may feel inclined to offer in connection with this preliminary study and in the light of their own experience in the field. Their reactions and recommendations will be welcome with a view to the improvement of the text in any subsequent edition.

It remains to be stated that while Unesco judges the publication of the present study to be useful, the ideas expressed are those of the author and should not be considered as Unesco's doctrine on the subject.

Contents

Introduction 11

I General principles 25
    1 Functional literacy and evaluation 25
    2 Evaluation of an experimental project 28
    3 Evaluation of an operational project 32
    4 External and internal evaluation 34

II Techniques and instruments 37
    1 Limitations 37
    2 Methods of investigation and sources of information 38
    3 Project information methods 46
    4 Studies of change 48
    5 Analysis of results 57

III Preliminary studies 67
    1 Objectives and scope 61
    2 Definition of objectives 62
    3 Feasibility 64
    4 Identification of programme content 67
    5 Action planning 71

IV Quantitative evaluation of results 77
    1 Objectives 77
    2 Scope 77
    3 Descriptive studies 78

    4 Comparative studies 79
    5 Explanatory studies 80

V Qualitative evaluation of results 83
    1 Objectives 83
    2 Scope 83
    3 Instruments 84
    4 Descriptive studies 87
    5 Comparative studies 88
    6 Explanatory studies 89

VI Evaluation of the impact of the logistic components of the project 95
    1 Objectives 95
    2 Scope 96
    3 Instruments 96
    4 Descriptive studies 98
    5 Explanatory studies 100

VII Evaluation of programme content 103
    1 Objectives 103
    2 Scope 103
    3 Instruments 108
    4 Descriptive studies 110
    5 Explanatory studies 112

VIII Evaluation of predicted changes 119
    1 Objectives and general methodology 119
    2 Scope 120
    3 Instruments 121
    4 Descriptive studies 123
    5 Comparative studies 124
    6 Explanatory studies 125

IX Global evaluation of the project 133
    1 Quantitative evaluation of results 133
    2 Qualitative evaluation of results 134
    3 Evaluation of the impact of logistic components of the project 138
    4 Evaluation of programme content 139
    5 Global evaluation of the project 139

Appendix 145
- Document 1: Register of participants 147
- Document 2: Monthly report 148
- Document 3: End-of-cycle report 150
- Document 4: Test of know-how (cotton programme) 151
- Document 5: Literacy scale 152
- Document 6: Course sheet 153
- Document 7: Dimensions, criteria and indicators for the evaluation of social, economic and psycho-cultural changes 155
- Document 8: List of hypotheses formulated for the global evaluation of EWLP 160

Select bibliography 165

Index 167

Introduction

Before turning to the structure of this guide, some clarification of the sense in which the terms incorporated in the title are interpreted by the author may be of use, namely, 'guide', 'practical', 'literacy' and 'evaluation'.

The concepts used

Guide

This work is not an instructional manual. The reader will not find in its pages the basic notions of sociology, psychology, pedagogy, economics or statistics which are necessary to evaluation. It will not teach laymen to become evaluators.

It is, however, a source of information on matters related to the evaluation of literacy projects. It will help the evaluator to find his bearings by reminding him of certain essentials at the appropriate moment, by proposing a wide range of options to him and by suggesting directions which he might take to perfect his work. Finally, it calls his attention to the hazards which eh may encounter, as identified during the global evaluation of the Experimental World Literacy Programme (EWLP) and during the author's own period in the field.

Practicality

A number of pages are devoted to the theoretical aspects of evaluation and contain tables, briefly annotated, in the explicit hope that certain projects will permit verification of the hypothesis that literacy action—

and functional literacy in particular—improves man's well-being and enables him to participate more fully in society, to master his natural environment more consciously and efficiently, and to increase his own productivity.

But above all the guide is intended to be practical, i.e. related to action and application. It is designed to lead the evaluator progressively from simple (Chapter IV) to complex (Chapter IX) operations, while placing emphasis on orderly and chronological procedures (particularly in Chapters I, II and III) and following both a chronological and a logical order in the presentation of the chapters devoted to the main fields covered by evaluation.

'Practical' does not, however, imply 'elementary'. The task of evaluation demands from at least some of the members of the responsible team the capacity to construct and manipulate instruments currently employed in sociology and pedagogy, and familiarity with basic statistical methods. It is for these specialists that the guide is intended.

The evaluator is thus guided step by step. Each chapter begins with a statement of the objectives of the field of evaluation in question, and then presents a wide range of actions which it may be possible —or interesting—to undertake, and among which the reader will choose according to his own purposes and the means at his disposal. The instruments required are described and sometimes presented more fully in the Appendix. Finally, each chapter proposes a list of hypotheses, the verification or invalidation of which should permit intervention during the progress of the project with a view to modifying those elements which the outcome of studies may have shown to be unsatisfactory.

Literacy work

All literacy programmes are now to a greater or lesser extent functional. Other published works, including Unesco publications, deal with the methodology of functional literacy, so that it does not require definition in these pages. Nevertheless, and for the reasons set out at the beginning of Chapter I, this guide lays emphasis on the functional literacy method, and its approach to the evaluation of the functional aspects of literacy training is conditioned by respect for the basic principles of this method.

On the other hand, project stimulators who do not truly apply the functional method will find here all that is necessary to enable them to plan the evaluation of their own activities correctly, since the guide is structured in such a way as to present the methods, actions, techniques and instruments of evaluation in three categories, which correspond to an order of increasing complexity.

Category A is intended for experts whose sole concern is with 'internal evaluation' (see Chapter I, Section 4), i.e. with quantification of the project in all its aspects, with verification of its harmonious evolution as a whole, with the control of results and with some measure of pedagogical experimentation; who are not particularly concerned with the method itself; and for whom the social or economic effects of literacy action are only of passing interest.

The pages or paragraphs of the guide which deal with this category are printed in the following type:

Study of this assembled information will allow of reasonable assumptions concerning the feasibility of literacy action in each village or human group.

Category B is intended more particularly for 'functional literacy' projects the sole purpose of which is internal evaluation. This form of evaluation is therefore covered in the guide by all the passages which deal with category A, together with a number of pages and paragraphs dealing with functional literacy, printed in the following type:

Sources of information are multiple and varied. There are accordingly a great many ways of carrying out investigations. We shall mention here those most frequently used.

Category C is intended for projects which seek to proceed beyond mere internal evaluation, and to examine the effects of literacy action in the social, economic and other fields.

The pages or paragraphs which deal with this category of 'external evaluation' are printed in the following type:

As in the preceding chapters, we shall mention a number of studies which may be undertaken to test simple hypotheses formulated on the basis of the list of assigned objectives.

Thus every literacy project, whatever its means, methods, or ambitions, will without difficulty find in the guide advice concerning appropriate actions, procedures and instruments, matching the desired degree of complexity.

Evaluation

The term 'evaluation', of course, is not employed in the restrictive sense of 'approximate determination of value or importance' but denotes, more precisely, a series of measurements made in connection with a literacy project for purposes of description, comparison, analysis, comprehension and explanation. We shall return in greater detail to this definition below, but must first turn to an important aspect of the guide, which concerns the notion of hypothesis.

The central hypothesis

Some readers may be shocked to find at the very outset of Chapter I of the guide the word 'hypothesis'—a term whose abstract connotations may well discourage those who seek practical solutions. But the admission—with which it would be difficult to disagree—that administrative action of any kind is designed solely to improve a given situation inevitably entails the formulation of a hypothesis, namely that the situation will be better than it was. The same is true of any educational project: in a given situation, it is generally assumed that the literacy action to be undertaken will lead to another situation judged in advance to be better. The evaluation of a literacy project involves the comparison of the current situation with two others: the initial situation; and the situation expected, anticipated and desired by the promoters of the project. For this evaluation to be fully effective, therefore, those responsible must be fully acquainted with: (a) the initial situation, hence the importance of preliminary studies (see Chapter II, Section 2: Methods of Investigation and Sources of Information, and Section 3: Project Information Methods); (b) the final situation, i.e. the situation at the conclusion of the project, as defined and anticipated by its promoters (see Chapter III, Section 2: Definition of Objectives, and Section 4: Identification of Programme Content).

To evaluate a literacy project is to take bearings at any given moment against these two points of reference, to calculate what has been done and what remains to be done: and this requires the adoption—or construction—of a central hypothesis for the project or, at least, failing this, familiarity with the challenge thrown out by those responsible for the literacy action involved.

This guide, intended to be as comprehensive as possible and to deal with the greatest number of foreseeable situations, is constructed around the central hypothesis of EWLP, which is set out in detail in

Chapter I. The choice of this hypothesis as a foundation stems from the fact that of all modern literacy methods, the functional method is certainly the most complex.

It is quite obvious, however, that this hypothesis, the verification of which mobilized for almost a year a large team of university graduates, lavishly equipped to analyse some 65,000 pages of documentation, is not within the reach of every undertaking. Every project must endeavour to construct its own hypothesis, based on the following example:

The project, the budget for which amounts to X, is intended to render N women in a given region literate, within two years, by providing them with a complete cycle of elementary education, together with training in home economics. Active methods of education will be employed for this purpose. Centres will be equipped with audio-visual equipment, material for self-teaching and radio receivers, since part of the teaching will be conducted in liaison with the national broadcasting service. It is believed that this action will have a beneficial influence on nutrition, hygiene, health and infant sickness and mortality rates.

On this basis the evaluator will prepare plans (see Chapter III, Section 5: Action Planning) concerning those aspects of the project on which its executants will require further information, specifically on: quantitative results (see Chapter IV); qualitative results (see Chapter V); logistics of the project (see Chapter VI); programme content (see Chapter VII); predicted changes (see Chapter VIII).

Also on the basis of the central hypothesis, the evaluator will select and endeavour to verify a few secondary hypotheses concerning, for example: optimum attendance; success in examinations; educational broadcasting; etc.

Each of the specialized chapters below contains a long list of such hypotheses, under the heading 'Explanatory Studies', while a further list containing hypotheses formulated during the global evaluation of EWLP will be found in the Appendix. Although they may provide useful guidance, they are included merely as examples, for of course no project can test them all, nor will their present formulation be necessarily suitable for retention.

Descriptive evaluation

In the chapters which follow, the reader will find a long list of 'variables' which lend themselves to measurement and which, because of their variations (i.e. the causes or effects of the trends which they reveal), reflect an evolving situation. The task of the evaluator is first to describe, then to analyse and finally to seek explanations of this situation. As far as literacy work is concerned, these variables will concern numbers of participants or of literacy centres involved, quantities of materials, results of examinations, and so on, which will be measured at certain critical stages of the project (at the outset and conclusion of courses, for example). The findings at given moments will be presented in the form of descriptive tables.

For example, Table 1-1 (Chapter IV, Section 3) will present the numbers of participants, in a given region or in the project as a whole, by sex and age group, at the moment when 'data' are collected (e.g. at the outset of the courses). The same data may be collected at the conclusion of the courses, so as to permit the calculation of, for example, drop-out ratios and so to describe the situation centre by centre, region by region and for the project as a whole. This drop-out ratio is both easy to calculate and highly significant. Thus when the drop-out ratio for the project as a whole is 30 per cent, but amounts to 60 per cent in one of the regions involved, it is clear that something unusual is happening in that region and that intervention (feedback) is called for.

The reader will observe that the data contained in Table 1-1 permit calculations which concern not only the group of participants as a whole, but also the two sexes and the different age groups separately. The advantage of such composite tables is that they permit the distribution of the data they contain in terms of several characteristics, which facilitates identification of the variable.

Chapters IV–VIII of the guide contain long lists of tables of data to be collected concerning the most interesting variables and their principal characteristics.

Obviously, no single project leader will collect data concerning all the variables indicated, nor prepare all the tables nor calculate all the indicators. The following pages present a broad range of possibilities of data collection, from which each project leader will select those which appear indispensable. Some projects will be more concerned with drop-outs or absenteeism, others with examination results or the results of tests in, say, arithmetic, and still others with logistical or pedagogical matters. The choice of themes will determine the choice of tables to be compiled. But the need to proceed with caution cannot be overstressed. It should be borne in mind that a decision to collect data concerning one variable alone will entail the collection of hundreds, perhaps thousands of figures for inclusion in dozens of tables, which will have to be verified, collated, compared, etc., the task involving hundreds of calculations. This decision should therefore only be taken after exhaustive debate between the different members of the team and after several experiments in a literacy centre. Account should be taken of the means at the disposal of the project in terms of qualified, competent staff, time, money and calculating equipment. What must be avoided is the collapse of the evaluation unit under an avalanche of data that no one will have the time to compare or examine, and with which the only calculation possible will be totalization.

Once selected and compiled, however, these tables will serve as the basis for 'descriptive studies', lists of which will be found in each fo the chapters dealing with the major fields to be covered by evaluation (see Contents).

Comparative and analytical evaluation

If evaluation is not to remain a sterile exercise confined to description, but is to become in its turn a means of impinging on the evolution of the project, the evaluator must proceed to the more complex tasks of comparing and analysing the results obtained during the initial, descriptive stage.

This might involve, for example, determining whether the project is evolving at the same speed and in the same manner everywhere. If certain centres are seen to be falling behind, remedial action will be necessary, since the project leaders will be budget-minded and disinclined to accept an increase in the costs of the operation. Conversely, if results are seen to be better in some centres than in others, it will be important to investigate the causes, so that the methods which yield these superior results can be extended throughout the entire project. But the mere observation of differences does not constitute sufficient grounds for claiming that the results observed are indeed different. Proof must be provided in the form of statistical analysis. This will involve the calculation of averages of series and variances, and the submission of results to other statistical tests (the 'Student' test, for example). The source of the difference may be identified by subjecting the results to still more tests, e.g. variance analysis. And where differences are shown to exist, it may be worth while to analyse the data in greater depth and to re-apply the tests, taking account this time of the characteristics of the variables examined. As a result, it may emerge that the difference in question is due to sex, age or the social or economic status of the participants, or to the place and time at which the courses concerned are held, etc.

The reader will have noted that at this stage the process of evaluation becomes more complex and requires more sophisticated data and a greater number of calculations. But it will also be noted that such evaluation provides those responsible for the direction and implementation of the project with more valuable information which —applied for the purposes of mid-course correction—should lead to better results from the same investments on the part of organizers and participants alike.

Each of the chapters dealing with the major fields to be covered by evaluation contains a list of suggested 'comparative studies' (see Contents).

Evaluation for the purposes of comprehension and explanation

The first two stages of the process of evaluation have made it possible to describe, compare and analyse various situations, and have perhaps incited project leaders to modify certain elements of the programme in the interests of better results.

The third stage is designed to enable the evaluator to understand what is happening. For in fact the teaching provided within the specific framework of the project, in a specific context and with specific means, is leading to changes in material, intellectual, psychological, cultural, social, economic and many other conditions. At the same time the population concerned is undergoing other learning processes not directly related to the process of becoming literate.

At this level the evaluator's role is to attempt to correlate some of the inputs of the project with the anticipated results of literacy training (outputs). He will certainly not be able to demonstrate that the increased agricultural production of a given region is the result of making its inhabitants functionally literate, since the effects of education are particularly difficult to measure. Diffuse in form and slow to materialize, these effects make themselves felt in the changing attitudes and behaviour of individuals and groups. And as is the case throughout the human sciences, it is virtually impossible to isolate and control all the variables involved.

But the evaluator can overcome this difficulty by constructing a large number of hypotheses, the testing of which will either confirm or invalidate his initial assumption. Let us suppose, for example, that he assumes the behaviour, technical know-how and ability to apply this know-how of workers who have undergone literacy training to be qualitatively superior to those of other adults. To test this basic hypothesis, he will construct a large number of secondary hypotheses, which will themselves be tested on two matched (control and experimental) samples of the workers concerned, and which may deal with absenteeism, appreciation by managerial staff (engineers and foremen) of the quality and quantity of the labour provided, the level of vocational knowledge, the adoption of viable practices, up-to-date procedures, more rational standards, or modern products (insectcides, fertilizers, etc.), and so forth.

It is certain that if all or most of these secondary hypotheses are verified, there would be reasonable grounds for considering that the qualitative improvement in question, which formed the basis of the initial assumption—and which indeed was anticipated by the promoters of the project in the central hypothesis—is a by-product of the functional literacy project. But this is as far as one may go.

Evaluation work of this kind necessitates the handling of delicate instruments and the utilization of sophisticated techniques, and consequently requires highly competent personnel. Only large-scale and well-endowed projects will be in a position to attempt this type of activity, which must, moreover, be subject to every appropriate scientific safeguard, while its conclusions should be treated with great circumspection.

Structure of the guide

Chapters I and II of the guide deal with the general principles of evaluation and the techniques and instruments proposed.

Chapter III deals with preliminary studies, and is more particularly aimed at projects which are not yet operational, where the organizers wish to make ample preparation for evaluation.

Chapters IV–VIII each deal with a major field to be covered by the evaluation of a literacy project.

The final chapter outlines a system of global evaluation and is followed by an Appendix containing eight model documents, and by a Bibliography and an Index.

As indicated above, the use of different type-faces in the printed text enables the reader to locate without difficulty those pages and passages the contents of which are particularly relevant to the project that concerns him.

The initial evaluative capacities and resources of certain projects may, however, be very limited, and it has been thought useful to set out below a number of brief considerations which may enable an inexperienced evaluation team to obtain maximum results from its activities.

The team leader should have a university degree in either pedagogical science or sociology, with a sound knowledge of the other subject. He should also be familiar with the main features of statistics and economics.

The team leader should be seconded by at least one assistant in each subproject or region, who will be responsible for the collection, verification and tabulation of relevant data and for liaison with the literacy centres. These assistants should have received adequate training to enable them to conduct surveys and to make simple statistical calculations (determination of averages, variances and correlation coefficients). Their level of schooling should for preference be above the first cycle of secondary education.

Staff at the project headquarters should include one or two 'mathematicians' responsible for collating the different tables compiled in the subprojects or regions and for making the more complex calculations required for purposes of research, together with specialists in pedagogy (for knowledge-testing), sociology (for the drafting of questionnaires and studies of the milieu), economics (for external evaluation), etc. This personnel should have received a complete secondary education.

Regional assistants for the project must be employed on a full-time basis. Specialized services may be obtained by arrangement with universities, possibly through contracts for the preparation of surveys, research activities, etc., by members of the teaching or research staff and, for the execution of these activities, by their students. Similarly, pedagogical research and experimentation may be entrusted to inspectors of education.

Activities which might be undertaken by a limited evaluation team are listed briefly below. The reader will find further explanations, together with definitions of the terms, techniques and instruments involved, in the pages of this guide.

Preliminary studies

At project headquarters
Planning of evaluation activities; preparation of instruments; training of regional assistants; agreement with universities concerning the organization of field surveys.

In the field
Baseline surveys and study of the milieu (with university participation); motivation surveys, research on programme content.

Studies concerning quantitative results

At the literacy centre
Numbers of participants present at each session are noted by the instructor in the monthly register, together with the number of absentees and the reasons for absence, indicated by code letters, such as:

H, health; W, work; F, traditional festivals or ceremonies; D, domestic reasons, children, etc.; T, travel, seasonal migration; C, climate, bad weather; N, unidentified; etc.

At the end of each month, and as a result of various simple calculations, the instructor may obtain the following statistics:

(a) number of sessions held during the month; (b) number of registrations at the beginning of the month; (c) total possible attendance (a) × (b); (d) total absences; (e) number of absences classified by reason for absence; (f) number of drop-outs during the month (by sex and age).

These statistics are transmitted monthly to the project headquarters and the regional office.

At the regional level
The regional office will use the information received from each centre to draw up the following tables: participants by sex and age group; participants by marital status; drop-outs by sex and age group; drop-outs by marital status; absences by sex and age group; absences by marital status; absences by reason for absence; drop-outs by reason for drop-out.

It will then be possible to establish the main indicators described in the guide (ratios of drop-outs, of attendance, of registration per programme, of time utilization) for the region (or programme) as a whole.

At project headquarters
It now becomes possible at project headquarters to undertake

the following tasks, *inter alia*: to totalize the different statistical tables received from regions or subprojects and to publicize them, with commentaries; to calculate, at the national level, the main indicators of yield; to make comparative and explanatory studies concerning the causation of drop-outs and absences, and measures for its elimination; to organize studies in greater depth (through sampling) on the basis of information provided by the lists of registration, involving for example the calculation of drop-out ratios in relation to the occupations of participants, the characteristics of instructors, the language used, tec.

Studies concerning qualitative results

At the literacy centre

Acceptance of literacy schedule; periodical testing in the main instructional techniques (reading, writing, dictation, arithmetic, applied arithmetic, vocational education, etc.); end-of-cycle testing; as the case may be, compilation of the results of each test according to sex, age, etc.

The tables listing these results are transmitted to the regional office.

At the regional level

Compilation, for each periodical test, of the results obtained in the centres, and calculation of percentage success rates by centre, sex and age group; compilation of the results of end-of-cycle tests in all the centres and calculation for the region of the different indicators of measurement of the knowledge acquired.

This information is transmitted to project headquarters.

At project headquarters

Comparison of the results received from the different regions; totalization of the regional tables and calculation of the indicators of measurement of knowledge acquired; analytical studies designed to provide the methodologists with numerical information concerning those elements of the various programmes of instruction which have produced poor results in periodical and end-of-cycle tests.

Evaluation of the impact of the logistic components of the project

At the literacy centre

Each instructor completes the 'course sheet' with the help of the regional assistant; the 'monthly report' is completed and transmitted to the regional office.

At the regional level

The regional assistant analyses the data from the 'course sheets' and the 'monthly reports' and draws up those of the tables mentioned in Chapter VI, Section 4, of the guide which are requested by project headquarters:

Distribution of courses according to location and timetable; distribution of courses according to participants/instructor ratios; distribution of instructors according to certain characteristics; teaching material and other assistance received; etc.

At project headquarters

Aggregation of the various tables received from regions or subprojects; comparative studies; calculation of certain average unit-costs (per participant registered or per successful participant, costs of creating and operating a literacy centre, costs per instructor, etc.).

Evaluation of programme content

This evaluation is of particular interest to methodologists who wish to carry out experiments with different methods, materials, etc. The evaluation unit may provide its own technical assistance (construction of samples, statistical calculations, etc.), but is not expected to take initiatives in the matter.

General principles I

1 Functional literacy and evaluation

The central hypothesis of functional literacy

The following considerations stem directly from the work of the Evaluation Unit of Unesco's Literacy Division, which in 1974 and 1975 carried out a global evaluation of the Experimental World Literacy Programme (EWLP). It will be recalled that this programme covered a period of ten years and involved more than a million participants in eleven countries, where 137 different literacy projects were put to the test. One feature of the undertaking—an exercise which proved extremely fruitful[1]—was an attempt to evaluate results, with the aim of verifying the central hypothesis of the functional literacy training on which EWLP was based. This hypothesis has been expressed in the following terms:

In favourable and well-ordered socio-economic conditions, a training process focused on development objectives and problems provides the individuals concerned with the intellectual and technical means for becoming more effective agents in the process of socio-economic development.

But should all literacy work be founded on the methods of functional literacy? The most recent major international meeting on the subject,

---

1. The technical documents produced by the EWLP evaluation team have not yet been published, but may be consulted in the documentation unit of the Literacy, Adult Education and Rural Development Division (ED/LAR) at Unesco Headquarters in Paris. These documents are listed in the Select Bibliography at the end of this volume.

held at Persepolis from 3 to 8 September 1975, issued the important Declaration of Persepolis, which states that:

Successes were achieved when literacy programmes were not restricted to learning the skills of reading, writing and arithmetic, and when they did not subordinate literacy to the short-term needs of growth unconnected with man. . . . These experiments, and in particular functional literacy programmes and projects, have made a valuable contribution to the common stock of practical methods in the field of literacy and basic education. Greater use should be made of them in future efforts. . . . The ways and means of literacy activities should be founded on the specific characteristics of the environment, personality and identity of each people. . . . The methods and material means should be diversified, flexible and suited to the environment and needs of the new literates, as opposed to a uniform and rigid model.

These extracts from the Declaration of Persepolis reveal the importance which its authors attached to the methods of functional literacy. Moreover, the Director-General of Unesco, Amadou-Mahtar M'Bow, in his address to the Meeting of Senior Officials of the Ministries of Education of the Twenty-five Least-developed Countries, held in Paris from 8 to 16 September 1975, stated that:

In the process of developing awareness of the realities of the national situation, and in the process of mastering knowledge and skills, the least developed countries should bear in mind the vital potential role of functional literacy schemes. As illiteracy rates are high in such countries, and as the ignorance of the majority of the adult population is a major obstacle to development, outstanding benefits may be derived from such schemes, the methods of which have gradually been developed as part of the Experimental World Literacy Programme adopted by the General Conference of Unesco in 1964 and carried out in co-operation with the United Nations Development Programme. Functional literacy, which is specifically designed to combine the promotion of literacy, as a means of direct access to the sources of knowledge, with meeting the need to involve the whole population in productive development activities without delay, provides a special link between education and work. However, its functional aspect may have a wider significance in that it helps to raise the level of awareness of the new literates and gives them a chance to work more effectively to improve their own situation.

The merits of functional literacy methods thus appear to have secured world-wide recognition. In fact, if we consider all the many literacy projects under way at present throughout the world—and no country, even if over-industrialized, is free from the scourge of illiteracy—it becomes clear that it is no longer possible for any literacy scheme to be other than totally or partially functional. This is why 'functional literacy' is referred to again and again in the following pages. Of all the literacy methods employed up to now, those of functional literacy have proved to be the most complex; and for this reason the documents proposed in this guide for the evaluation of functional literacy programmes may be adapted to suit simpler methods of literacy training, by reducing their scope or eliminating what are considered to be unnecessary details.

Major fields of evaluation

Global evaluation of a functional literacy programme amounts to verification of the central hypothesis set out above. Since verification of each element of the hypothesis calls for a series of specific evaluations which, taken together, permit assessment of its validity as a whole, the evaluation of individual literacy projects can, if provided with appropriate means, include attempts to evaluate the central hypothesis of functional literacy, and thus contribute to the overall assessment of this method of education.

In other words, the process of determining whether a given project meets its assigned objectives amounts to verification of the different elements of the central hypothesis, by ascertaining:

Whether the 'socio-economic conditions' of the project are indeed 'favourable and well-ordered' (by means of baseline surveys, feasibility studies and investigations of the logistic support received by literacy centres, etc.). Chapters III and VI of this guide cover these questions.

Whether the 'training process' (programmes, methods, curricula) is indeed 'focused on development objectives' (by verification of the 'functional' aspect of the training provided). This is covered by Chapter VII.

Whether the project 'provides the individuals concerned with "adequate" intellectual and technical means' (by measurement of the quantitative and qualitative results achieved by participants). This is the subject of Chapters IV and V.

Whether 'the individuals concerned become more effective agents in the process of socio-economic development' of the social unit to which they belong (by measurement of predicted changes). This is covered by Chapter VIII.

Thus the major tasks of an evaluation unit might comprise: project feasibility studies; research aimed at identification of programme content; evaluation of quantitative results obtained from the system; evaluation of attainments, in terms not only of literacy, but also of technical, vocational, social, economic and other knowledge and skills; evaluation of cultural, social, economic, technological and other transformations resulting from the project, and comparison of actual with predicted changes.

These basic terms of reference may be adopted for the evaluation of experimental and operational projects alike, although the methods and instruments employed will be less complex in the latter case.

2 Evaluation of an experimental project

Planning

Experimental projects should be subjected to particularly searching scrutiny, and their planning will of necessity be highly complex. It is essential to plan the majority of the experiments envisaged before the programme of training is launched, since any conclusions drawn from surveys or experiments mounted after training has begun will almost invariably suffer from the constraints imposed by the use of *ex post facto* data and from the impossibility of exercising control over all the variables involved. On the other hand, a well-prepared experimental plan will make it possible to conduct several experiments simultaneously with the same groups, provided that the participants are selected and matched with the greatest care in order to eliminate as many 'parasite' variables as possible.

Constitution of groups

Experimental projects are designed to determine the type of teaching which is best suited to the assigned objectives, which can be dispensed with the greatest speed and which presents the least difficulties to all participants. Since these projects are designed for expanded application to the whole population of broad geographical areas (or to large economic or social groups), they must be instantly adaptable to take account of individual differences within the groups concerned. Any secondary effects caused by the multiple variable of 'individual characteristics' must therefore be eliminated from the planned experiments.

This may be achieved by constructing nine, sixteen or twenty-five groups of participants (square numbers are of great use in such experiments), the members of which should be closely matched according to basic individual characteristics, such as sex and age, professional qualifications and seniority, etc. (for economic programmes), or number of children, living standards, etc. (for social or women's programmes). In this way, any variations occurring between the different groups may be assumed to be independent of the individual characteristics of the persons involved in the experiment. These individual characteristics may, however, serve on occasion as explanatory variables (for purposes of intra-group comparisons).

Stages of the experimental project

We shall confine ourselves here to an enumeration of the different stages and of the means of evaluation required in each case, indicating the chapters in which the reader will find relevant information concerning survey methods, instruments and their utilization, and the modes of analysis proposed or recommended.

Definition of the programme. The objectives of the project should be very clearly defined, if possible in quantified terms. This will involve the examination of official documents, discussions with the responsible technicians and administrators, and recourse to expert opinion (see Chapter III, Section 2).

Feasibility studies. It is here necessary to determine whether the political will to encourage and support literacy action exists at the regional or local level, whether the populations concerned are sufficiently motivated, whether financial resources exist, whether the human resources (instructors) are adequate; and to identify the environmental factors which will militate in favour of or against the project. This will involve, in addition to the activities mentioned above, motivation surveys and investigations of the milieu, as described in Chapter III, Section 3.

Identification of programme content. In order to ensure that the contents of the programme of training will be 'functional', i.e. adapted to the population concerned, it will be necessary:

To identify the motivations, desires, aspirations and interests of the prospective participants as far as education, apprenticeship and the improvement of their vocational skills are concerned.

To list the vocational-technical, socio-economic or other problems which may retard or obstruct the desired social or economic development.

To evaluate the present level of intellectual and technical knowledge of the population concerned.

To list the capacities or aptitudes required if the participants are to master the identified problems or obstacles.

The research required may involve: baseline surveys and the study of development plans; discussions with development authorities; motivation surveys and the investigation of interests; study of technical monographs.

Description of these will be found in Chapter III, Section 4.

Pedagogical evaluation. This process will depend upon a certain number of specific indicators of the quantitative and qualitative yields of the process of education, covering such subjects as drop-out and wastage ratios, success in final examinations, the results of periodical tests, etc. The methods and instruments to be used are described in Chapters IV and V.

Evaluation of acquired technological knowledge and abilities. The task here is to measure the results of technical education at three levels: theoretical knowledge, practical know-how and application. This type of measurement requires the construction of tests and the utilization of interviews, expert judgements and observation sheets, all of which are discussed in Chapters V and VIII.

Evaluation of anticipated socio-economic changes. This stage, which is that of terminal evaluation, is the most necessary, if not the most important, because it will determine whether the objectives fixed at the outset of the project—to effect favourable transformations of the milieu through functional literacy action—have indeed been attained. It may be noted, however, that the duration of the experimental projects is generally too short, while too little time is left between the completion of the evaluation of a project and its extension, in modified form and as an operational project, over a whole area.

It will therefore be necessary to plan for an extension of the project, which will initially be slow and limited, thus allowing for the measurement of the anticipated social, cultural and economic changes in the groups receiving literacy training. The results of these measurements will indicate whether it is necessary to modify the content of the teaching before extending the action still further.

Conclusions

All the data collected during the evaluation of the experimental project will be correlated by use of appropriate statistical methods, so as to permit the team responsible for the execution of the project to find answers to a number of questions, among the most important of which may well be the following:

What are the reasonable objectives which may be assigned to the project in view?

What concept of literacy training is best suited to the realization of the project?

What are the minimum conditions of feasibility of the project (in political, ecological, financial and human terms)?

What contents of teaching programmes are most likely to satisfy both the desires of the populations concerned and the concern of the technicians to see the elimination of certain obstacles to development?

What learning methods are best suited to the adults concerned; what is the most useful educational material; what are the most suitable techniques; and what is the minimum time-span to produce the best results in terms of quantity and depth of knowledge, quality of know-how, and importance and quality of application of this know-how?

What is the best way of constituting groups, and what personal characteristics should be sought in participants to obtain the best results?

What is a reasonable estimate of the unit costs of extending the action beyond the experimental stage?

What personal characteristics should be sought in instructors and supervisors to obtain the best results?

What strategy should be adopted for the extension of the project (planning in time and space, motivation campaigns among the population and the authorities, organization of participation, etc.)?

What difficulties may be expected during the period of extension of the project?

3 Evaluation of an operational project

Objectives

This type of evaluation comprises first and foremost a system of control making it possible to determine in the most impartial manner possible whether the quantitative objectives assigned at the outset have been attained; and by means of a series of scientific measurements, to identify the factors which militate in favour of, or in opposition to, literacy action. Work in the field can thus be followed and checked in both its quantitative and its qualitative aspects.

The data collected should make it possible to reply to the following questions:

Is the struggle to eradicate illiteracy developing, and is it attaining the planned objectives?

Is the political and socio-economic context of the literacy action well-ordered and favourable, and is the population concerned suitably informed and motivated?

Do the instructional technologies[1] involved match the planned objectives?

Have the participants really been rendered functionally literate, and are they now directly involved in the economic, social and cultural development of the nation?

The answers to these questions necessitate the establishment of a system for the periodic collection of data by a team of qualified evaluators.

Description of the evaluation system

Whereas it was necessary at the experimental stage to collect data at the level of individuals, it is sufficient to collect data at the group level to ascertain whether an operational project is proceeding satisfactorily. Three types of control should be applied:

1. The term 'instructional technology' is used in preference to 'programme' to denote a complete series of sequences delivered over a specific period to the same groups of participants whose training has begun at the same time (batches), and designed to teach a specific technology (e.g. rice-growing, sugar-beet cultivation, cotton-growing, home economics, child care, automobile maintenance and repair, masonry, etc.)

General principles

Statistical control. Data collection should be thorough and conducted at regular intervals. At the local and regional levels, data may be processed by the instructors and supervisors; at project headquarters, processing should be carried out by computer if possible.

Pedagogical control. Data collection should be thorough and conducted at regular intervals. Data will be processed at the local level and analysed at the regional level.

Control of socio-economic impact. This control must be carried out at project headquarters, intermittently and by random sampling.

Statistical control

The basic statistical data, collected exhaustively and—as we have seen—at the group and no longer the individual level, will be processed if possible by computer, to extract information concerning: the geographical situation: province, district, locality; the group: course of training followed, cycle, number of applications, group identification number; the participants: number of initial and additional registrations by sex and age-group; attendance and drop-out; results, number of candidates entered for final examinations, number of successful candidates; teaching material distributed; number of visits by the supervisor; number of sequences taught (instructors' reports); results of weekly tests.

This information will be drawn from the 'monthly report' (see Appendix, Document 2), the 'course sheet' (Appendix, Document 6) which is drawn up a month after the beginning of the course of instruction, and the 'end-of-cycle report' (see Appendix, Document 3). The models referred to should be adapted to suit the types of treatment and analysis selected for the project in question. Provision may be made for aggregation by region, by executing agency, by instructional technology, etc.

Pedagogical control

Two types of pedagogical evaluation may be envisaged for verification of the effectiveness of courses of instruction:

First, weekly or fortnightly tests constructed in advance and included in the material supplied to the instructor for each sequence of the instructional technology in question. Applied by the instructors, these tests will provide them with an indication of the progress of participants in each component of the programme, together with information which will enable them to orientate their teaching activities.

Second, periodic and terminal tests, the results of which will serve as the basis for the award of certificates to participants who have obtained the critical score. These tests will preferably be applied by the supervisors. Sample studies of their results may be made at project headquarters with a view to revising the primers used by participants, other teaching material or the selection of instructors.

Control of socio-economic and cultural impact

This control may be effected by sampling of participants who have successfully completed the full programme of literacy training. The assumed evolution will be measured by means of a series of easily determined indicators. This process should permit an assessment of the success of the literacy action in such spheres as the acquisition of know-how, the capacity to obtain and communicate information, participation in social and political life, ability to plan, to organize and to solve day-to-day problems, etc.

4. External and internal evaluation

Irrespective of whether the project to be evaluated is experimental or operational, a distinction should be made between two types of evaluation. The first involves the comparison of actual results achieved by the programme with its assigned objectives (social, economic, cultural, etc.) within a specific framework (financial, geographic, human, etc.). It is related to global perspectives of change which go beyond the limits of the literacy action itself, and will be called 'external evaluation', corresponding to the final term of the central hypothesis of functional literacy. This type of evaluation will be used for comparisons with other types of training, or to assess the economic and social costs of literacy action, and is beyond the capacities of small-scale projects the human and material resources of which are limited.

'Internal evaluation' is directly related to the methodology applied. It may be conducted not only after but during the implementation of a project, and may serve purposes of adjustment, since the immediate examination of the results of such evaluation can lead to feedback intervention at all levels of the methodological schedule adopted. Internal evaluation will thus be concerned with: programme content and presentation (teaching materials); programme organization (progression, duration, integration, educational practice, etc.); the recruitment and training of instructors; the constitution of groups; etc.

If the system of evaluation we have described is to be fully effective, the techniques and instruments employed must be accompanied by a maximum of scientific guarantees. In Chapter II we shall endeavour to propose methods which should permit the construction of highly reliable instruments, while stressing the need, wherever possible, to use simple devices and to follow scientific procedures.

Techniques and instruments II

1 Limitations

The instruments of evaluation are those which are used by sociologists and psychologists. The beginner can thus consult any manual of sociology or psychology to learn how to carry out a survey, conduct an interview, construct a questionnaire or test, take samples, prepare an experimental plan, etc. However, a study of the techniques and instruments adopted by the different evaluation teams of the Experimental World Literacy Programme (EWLP) and of the difficulties encountered in the field by the evaluators of EWLP projects leads us in the following pages to offer some suggestions concerning better utilization of these techniques and instruments.

First and foremost, we must accept the fact that in the social sciences, absolute certainty belongs to the realm of the desirable rather than the possible. Yet the planning of research leading to the evaluation of literacy projects will involve an attempt to prove that the assumed interrelations between observed phenomena are due to selected factors which are presumed to be the 'causes' of changes noted in the dependent variable which is under consideration. We should admit at once that mastery of all the variables which act directly or indirectly on the phenomenon with which we are concerned must present enormous difficulties. And since the sources of uncertainty dominate wherever the causes of variations defy total control, we should be extremely cautious in our attempts to explain phenomena on the basis of the results of one experimental project.

As a means of keeping this element of uncertainty within

reasonable bounds, we cannot recommend too highly extreme rigour in the construction of an experimental plan or instrument, in the collection and processing of data, in control operations at all levels, in the detection (and if possible, suppression) of sources of uncertainty, in the selection of samples, in the application of statistical tests, etc.

The techniques and instruments of evaluation will be examined below in the chronological order in which they might be used during the evaluation of a literacy project, first for the collection of information, next for the processing of this information and, finally, for the investigation and analysis of changes.

2 Methods of investigation and sources of information

Sources of information are multiple and varied. There are accordingly a great many ways of carrying out investigations. We shall mention here those most frequently used.

A Documentary records

The evaluator will do well to begin by collecting and assembling all the printed documentation deemed necessary at the outset of the exercise. Familiarity with the contents of these documents will render the subsequent discussions more effective. The following list of documents to be consulted is not exhaustive, and is provided merely as an example. Documents should always be carefully referenced (place of origin, author, title, page number and name of the person with whom the document is deposited).

Statistical yearbooks: demography, health, the economy and education.

Social and economic development plans, national and regional.

Operational plans prepared by the public or private authorities responsible for development in the regions to be covered by literacy action: State or private enterprises, international organizations (UNDP, FAO, ECE, etc.).

Legislative texts.

Political speeches.

Budgets.

Geographical, economic, demographic, climatological and other maps.

Economic, sociological and other studies of the regions concerned.

Documents dealing with adult education.

Press cuttings.

Documents, *résumés* or photocopies, should be classified in an orderly manner for easy reference (see in this connection Classification System of Documents of the Experimental World Literacy Programme).[1]

B Discussions

Once the evaluator has familiarized himself with the documentation concerning subjects related to literacy action, he may begin the process of discussions with the representatives, at different levels, of organizations and other bodies likely to be concerned with the problems of literacy. These discussions will deal for the most part with:

The political decision to undertake literacy action.
The definition of objectives: population, area, social, cultural or economic objectives to be reached.
The forms of assistance proposed (financial, material, manpower) at headquarters, regional and local levels.
The collaboration envisaged (with administrations, development bodies, research institutes, universities, etc.).
Problems related to the types of education to be provided (mainly discussed with the Ministry of Education).
Programme content (with technicians from the agricultural, health, industrial and other sectors).
The organization of action and support in the localities where groups are to be constituted (to be discussed with administrations and non-governmental organizations).
Etc.

Since most of these discussions will be of interest first and foremost to the senior official of the project, they should be organized jointly by the project leader and the evaluator.

At this point the evaluation team should be in possession of all relevant information concerning:

The intensity of the political will to organize and sustain literacy action, which should be reflected in action at the administrative level.
The limits of the geographical area or social or economic sector to be covered by the literacy action, and the identification of the population concerned.
The characteristics of this population and of the geographical or administrative area concerned (demography, ethnology, sociology, culture, education, economy, infrastructure).
The objectives, quantified if possible, of the literacy action to be

---

1. M. T. Bazany and R. Couvert, in *Literacy Documentation*, Vol. II, No. 2, Tehran, International Institute for Adult Literacy Methods, April, 1973.

undertaken, and the identity of the development bodies in collaboration with which it will be implemented.

The economic or social objectives assigned by the development bodies (State or private) to the area in question and to its population.

The financial, human and material resources of national, regional, private or international origin to be made available to the project.

Organic links between the project and national or regional authorities, the sponsoring Ministry, private or public development bodies, and the non-governmental organizations from which support may be expected.

The organizational chart of the literacy project, and the specific function of the evaluation unit, as well as the definition, as precise as possible, of its assigned objectives and of the human and material resources at its disposal.

The main elements of the curriculum, and the teaching methods which are considered desirable, which are recommended or which are mandatory.

C   Field visits

Once the prior information has been collected, the theoretical objectives determined and the evaluation team constituted, it will be time to make contact with the population and the area concerned. Field visits will make it possible to determine whether the literacy action envisaged is in fact realizable, and should be concerned with both the physical and the sociological environment; and with the population itself, its awareness and receptivity, motivations and interests. Particular efforts should be made to visit those parts of the area which are least-favoured and least favourable from the points of view of accessibility, infrastructure, patterns and standards of living, technological culture, education, health and the acceptance of strangers.

These visits should achieve a popular response if accompanied by action designed to promote favourable attitudes towards literacy. They will also enable the evaluation team to draw up a map of the region,[1] containing for each village or scattered community, information concerning:

The infrastructure: means of access and available premises.

---

1. Emphasis is laid in these pages on rural projects, which are certainly the most complex, but the guidance provided may easily be adapted to industrial or women's projects.

The level of education of the population: presence of possible instructors.
Potential contribution from the community in terms of time and labour allowing for local levels and standards of living.
Motivation of the population: interests, participation.
Types of local assistance: political, moral and material.
Study of this assembled information will allow of reasonable assumptions concerning the feasibility of literacy action in each village or human group.

Questionnaires and observation sheets

After selecting experimental and control villages (see below, Section 4, B), the evaluation team will carry out further far-reaching surveys designed to provide better and more detailed knowledge of the population which is to receive literacy training, and to permit: (a) determination of the content of most of the components of the programme of teaching; and (b) selection and shaping of indicators of measurement of anticipated changes.

This process will mainly involve the use of questionnaires and observation sheets. Manuals of sociology contain an abundance of information concerning the former, but we have set out below a number of considerations which should enable the evaluator of literacy programmes to draw maximum benefit from this important method of investigation.

Form

With regard to the form of the questionnaire, it should be pointed out at the start that the questioning should in no way resemble an official 'interrogation'. It is thus preferable, wherever possible, to replace direct questioning by a process of discreet observation. The investigator should also refrain from using tape-recorders when working among people unfamiliar with audio-visual equipment.

The length of the questionnaires or the duration of conversations are not criteria on which their quality can be established. The questionnaire is only a means to an end, and excessive length, due to exaggerated ambition on the part of the investigators, will necessitate recourse to a large number of additional instruments. True criteria for the length of a questionnaire, apart from its cost, are the amount of interest and the degree of fatigue which it provokes among those questioned. Before they are applied, therefore, questionnaires should be tested on individuals with similar socio-cultural or professional characteristics.

The printed layout of the questionnaire is relatively immaterial. What is essential is to elicit replies which provide the required information, and this depends more on the skill of the questioner than on the wording of the questions themselves. Ideally a questionnaire might well consist of a mere list of numbers, together with the corresponding replies of the subjects. Each questionnaire should, however, be accompanied by a set of instructions to which the investigator, even if he has received prior training, may refer. These will indicate at least: the object and duration of the survey; the means and methods used, including the questionnaire; the order and—in cases where subtle shades of thought are required—the form in which certain questions should be posed, although it should be stressed once again that a good investigator is conducting a conversation and not drafting a police report; reminders, where appropriate, that where the question itself does not provoke a sufficiently precise or qualified response, the investigator should add his own appreciation of the reply given in so far as the latter is inadequate.

Content

As far as the content of the questionnaire is concerned, the procedure set out below is perhaps a lengthy one, but it is efficient, being based on an approach that is logical, economic and chronological. It comprises the following stages:

Detailed definition of the objectives of the survey. This should include the long-term objective of the exercise and, therefore, the operational action envisaged if the results of the survey are favourable. Knowledge at the outset of the distant project towards which the survey is directed will act as an incentive to greater creativity on the part of the investigator.

Investigation and definition of the main lines of inquiry to be adopted by the survey. Let us take the example of a survey designed to evaluate the changes that may be expected in a society subjected to functional literacy training. Since the purpose of this training is to provide the population concerned with the intellectual and technical means of modifying their mental attitudes and their patterns and standards of living, the survey should be concerned with the subjects' determination: to change; to acquire knowledge; to be able to plan, to organize and to solve problems; to obtain, communicate and disseminate information; to participate; to acquire know-how; to take action; to improve their living standards; to welcome progress.

In fact, by taking positive steps in each of these directions, the worker who is rendered literate should be contributing to the overall transformation of the milieu, which is the ultimate objective of the literacy action.[1]

Investigation of significant criteria for measuring anticipated changes in each of the main trends covered by the survey; this involves making an inventory of the different types of action, behaviour and attitude that may be observed (and if possible measured by indicators or indices) as significant and objective expressions of the anticipated changes. At this point visits to the fields and to the place of work of the participants, discussions and the study of technical monographs assume their full importance. Document 7 in the Appendix to this guide proposes a list of criteria for a programme of functional literacy training for mine workers.

Initial selection of indicators for the measurement of anticipated changes. This involves choosing from among a number of indicators relevant to each criterion only those best suited to demonstrate and determine the validity of the selected hypothesis. These indicators should be representative and objective, as well as easily identifiable and measurable. They should, in fact, possess the characteristics required of a sound test: validity, reliability and sensitivity. They will be utilized at two levels—some of them for purely descriptive purposes, and others for explanatory purposes and the identification of dependent variables.

The first task will be to draw up a list of the statistical calculations which are necessary to achieve the demonstration for which the questionnaire is being constructed. For example, the intermediate study of a literacy project for workers is designed on the one hand to produce a balance-sheet of the pedagogic results of teaching and to identify the obstacles that may have impeded the acquisition of knowledge according to plan; and on the other hand to determine whether

1. These nine directions were defined as essential after an analysis conducted as part of the global evaluation of EWLP (see Technical Document VI, referred to in Section 1 of the Bibliography).

economic and social changes have taken place. Among the data such a study demands will be: the results of weekly tests; the results of the final test; the personal characteristics of the workers in the experimental and control groups selected as samples; the social, economic, occupational and other changes which have taken place since the preliminary survey.

The above list is not exhaustive, our intention being merely, by means of this example, to throw light on the procedure to be followed and not to follow this particular study through in every detail.

The evaluator will then prepare tables for the collection of the necessary data in the form required for statistical processing. In this way he will obtain a standard size of units and a finite classification of groups of data. From these tables he will select an initial list of indicators which it will be the purpose of the questionnaire to obtain.

Detailed formulation of the hypotheses the verification of which is the object of the intended survey. The many technical documents resulting from the global evaluation of EWLP[1] contain a great number of such hypotheses, from which we shall borrow the following example.

Let us suppose that we wish to verify that literacy action has had a favourable influence on the output of a group of workers and that the latter have become 'more effective agents in the process of socio-economic development' (the central hypothesis of functional literacy), in other words that their training has enabled them *inter alia* to improve their professional know-how at the level of production. We must therefore verify whether their skills and working habits have been improved. If we take the improvement of working habits as a criterion, we may select, as items for measurement, the good care of the machinery, the degree of cleanliness of machines and their surroundings, respect for safety standards and absenteeism—four indicators for the criterion of 'improved working habits'.

For the validity of the hypothesis to be proved beyond doubt, the processing of the relevant data must show:

That both the control group and the experimental group were homogeneous as far as variables were concerned, before the programme of training was launched (hence the test of homogeneity of variants for the variables of each group).

That the two groups are no longer homogeneous after the programme

---

1. See Select Bibliography.

of training (hence the test of homogeneity of variants on data collected after the programme).

That the indicators retained for each criterion have developed in a favourable direction and that the change reflected in the measurements before and after the programme is significant (this involves significance-testing of differences between averages, for each indicator).

That there is a correlation between the improvement in the working habits of workers in the experimental group and the results obtained either in the final test or in the weekly tests of technical knowledge acquired as a result of the programme of training.

In order to make the necessary statistical calculations we must be in possession of a certain amount of data concerning each worker in the control group, which may be collected in a variety of different ways (tests, questionnaires, consultation of factory statistics, etc.). These data might, for example, be related to: the number of greasing operations carried out on the machines per day or per week (questionnaire); the degree of cleanliness of the machine (observation); the number of cleaning operations carried out on the surroundings of the machines (questionnaire); the number of days of absence, and the causes, during the month (questionnaire and consultation of factory statistics); the number of accidents, and their causes, during the month (idem); the observance of safety regulations (observation and questionnaire); the results of final tests (tests, project statistics); the results of weekly tests (idem); etc.

Thorough investigation of the plans, methods and statistical instruments to be employed shows that it will be necessary to identify modifications affecting a certain number of specific indicators, and that this will involve the on-the-spot collection of basic data. After deciding on the simplest and most effective form to be given to such data, the investigators will select the most appropriate method of collection (observation, interviews, questionnaires, etc.).

Construction of the questionnaire. When the list of all the data to be collected by questionnaire has been drawn up, the questionnaire itself is constructed according to the classical rules. The method described above ensures that it will contain all the necessary questions but no others. This enables us to reply to our earlier question concerning the length of the questionnaire: it will be long enough to contain all the questions that cannot be answered otherwise but no longer, since wherever possible the quest for information has been transferred to other instruments. The investigator will be equally certain of having omitted nothing of importance, while the prior preparation of data-collection tables will have established the form of the replies.

E   Technical monographs

Every functional literacy programme will include an element of technical training, which may cover subjects as varied as the care of new-born infants, the cultivation of tomatoes, weaving and spinning, or safety in mines.

In each case specialists will be invited to prepare technical monographs, and it will be the task of the educationists attached to each project to translate these technical messages into language which is immediately accessible to the participants in the courses of training.

3   Project information methods

Publicity for the results of surveys and studies conducted by an evaluation unit is essential, for it should not be forgotten that these activities are frequently carried out at the request of one or other of the specialized services attached to the project. There is a constant need, on the part of the teams responsible for planning and execution, for exact information concerning, on the one hand, the 'raw material' (i.e. the population concerned as it evolves) and, on the other hand, the results of continuous evaluation of their theoretical or practical day-by-day work with the instructional material.

It is thus incumbent on the evaluation team both to furnish the project leaders with the means of keeping the project workers and the public at large informed, and to constitute a sort of pictorial record of the project portraying each important moment of its evolution. Two types of documentation are involved: monographs dealing with the results of baseline, interim and final surveys; and statistical-type publications containing annotated tables covering the results of work bearing on the main indicators of measurement of change (for basic indicators, see Section 4 below).

A   Baseline surveys

The results of baseline surveys might form the subject of an initial major publication, comprising under one cover both a statement of the objectives of the project, together with a description of its organization and its operational plan, and a portrayal of the area and population concerned before the literacy project was launched. The contents of this document might include:

The project
Objectives, internal organization, operational plan.

Description of the area and population concerned
Physical environment: (a) delimitation of the area (urban, rural), maps, distances; (b) physical geography (plains, mountains, sea-coast, etc.); (c) climate (implications for the project).
Social environment: (a) population, demography (emigration, seasonal migrations, immigration); (b) type of habitat: concentrated, dispersed (distances); (c) religion, culture; (d) language (national, mother-tongue, dialect); (e) social organization: administrative, traditional (real and apparent centres of decision); (f) associations (political, cultural, women's organizations, sport, etc.); (g) social equipment (town hall, meeting rooms): (i) hospitals (sickness and mortality statistics: adults and children); (ii) education (schools, libraries, level of literacy and ratios of school attendance); (iii) leisure activities; (h) utilization of mass media (newspapers, radio, television, cinema); (i) etc.
Economic environment: (a) infrastructure: (i) access: roads (condition, bridges, beds), rail, sea or river, air; (ii) running water; (iii) electricity; (iv) postal and telephone services; (v) banks; (b) brief outline of production (primary, secondary, tertiary, exports, imports, etc.); (c) development projects, rural extension, etc.; (d) commerce and handicrafts; (e) etc.
Professional environment of participants: (a) economic sector (rural, agricultural, industrial, cottage industry); (b) main and ancillary productions of the firm or enterprise (agricultural, industrial, artisans); (c) jobs performed by participants; (d) working environment (heat, noise, cold, humidity, etc.); (e) industrial accidents and morbidity; (f) vocational training; (g) promotion opportunities; (h) welfare assistance; (i) trade unions; (j) etc.

Characteristics of participants and groups
Samples: method of sampling, degree of representation, size, estimated rate of mortality, degree of accuracy, strata selected.
Groups: size, location, homogeneity of age and of occupation, participants/instructor ratio.
Instructors and supervisors: personal characteristics.
Participants: personal characteristics (age, sex, marital status, professional status, salary, language, level of literacy, etc.).
Material conditions of literacy training: locality, time-table, frequency and duration of classes, premises, furniture.
Programme components of each cycle, time-table.
Etc.

The results of interim and final surveys should be published in the same form in order to permit valid comparisons.

The other technical services of the project may also publish their own documents, such as programmes, technical monographs, etc.

B   Statistical tables

These tables, which should be published at regular intervals, and if possible monthly, might include statistics, both partial (by province or by instructional technology) and global, covering: absenteeism, by sex, age and cause; drop-out, by sex, age and cause; results of interim tests; results of end-of-cycle tests.

4   Studies of change

The evaluation of a literacy project is to a great extent a matter of predicting, perceiving, measuring and analysing changes. We have seen above how changes may be predicted. Their perception and measurement require new instruments, and involve the application of specific indicators applied within experimental groups.

A   Basic indicators

EWLP formulated a standardized data reporting system which has proved its worth and which might usefully be employed for our own purposes. In the description which follows, the numbering of paragraphs has been simplified in comparison with the system followed in the relevant EWLP documents.

Turnover in programmes

1. *Ratio of registration in the programme.* This indicator is calculated by number of participants originally registered, over number of places available in the project planners.

    The period of registration will depend on local conditions, but should not exceed one month from the beginning of the groups' activities. If, however, this period is longer, the term 'participants originally registered' includes participants registered on the date of constitution of the batch.

    'Number of places available' means the number planned by the project for a specific programme at a specific stage of that programme. For each programme, this indicator is calculated at the end of the first month following registration. In the case of mixed groups, the age and sex of each participant registered or initially registered should be provided.

Techniques and instruments

2. *Ratio of drop-outs.* This indicator is calculated on a monthly basis on the number of participants of the batch who have abandoned the cycle at a given stage of the programme during the month, over the number of participants in the batch in question.

    A drop-out is a person who has been absent from a course for an entire month, or who is so regarded by the instructor. When registration continues beyond the date limit referred to above (additional registrations), the ratio of drop-outs is also calculated with regard to the total number of participants registered (initial plus additional registrations) at the end of the month in question.

3. *Ratio of attendance.* This indicator is calculated as actual daily attendance of participants registered at the beginning of the month in question, over the figure obtained by multiplying the planned number of daily courses by the number of registered participants at the beginning of the month (additional registrations during the month are not taken into account).

4. *Ratio of time-utilization.* This indicator is calculated by sessions actually held during the month in question, over planned daily sessions.

5. *Ratio of coverage.* This indicator is calculated as the number of places available at the beginning of the programme, over the estimate of potential participants.

    The number of places available is the number envisaged by the authors of the project for a given population and for a specific programme. The estimate of potential participants is the number of persons who meet the conditions for participation as defined by the authors of the project (age, sex, occupation, level of literacy, etc.) within a given section of the population, e.g. cotton planters aged between 14 and 15.

6. *Ratio of participation in final test.* This indicator is calculated as the number of members of the batch actually tested at the end of a given cycle of a given programme, over the total number of members of the batch. In the case of additional registrations, the ratio is also calculated as the number actually tested, over the total number of registered participants in the corresponding cycle of the programme.

Indicators of measurement of acquired skills

7. *Literacy skills achieved.* This indicator is calculated as the percentage of originally registered illiterates who, at the end of a given cycle or programme and having successfully passed objective tests, are declared to be literate. The critical scores and

systems of marking for the tests will have been determined by a group of experts *in situ*.

The construction of standard tests to permit assessment of attainments in the four following fields is recommended: (a) basic arithmetic; (b) ability to apply arithmetic to specific occupational tasks; (c) ability to read with comprehension (e.g. technical handbooks); (d) ability to express and convey a simple message in writing.

8. *Acquisition of occupational/technical knowledge.* This indicator is calculated as the percentage of originally registered illiterates who, at the end of a given cycle or programme, successfully pass the corresponding aptitude tests, criteria for which will have been determined by those responsible for the project. These tests should correspond to the subjects included in the programme of teaching and to the objectives fixed for the participants (minimum level of vocational/occupational knowledge).

9. *Acquisition of socio-economic knowledge*

10. *Acquisition of knowledge in health, hygiene, nutrition, infant welfare, etc.* The acquisition of knowledge in the fields covered by these two indicators will be measured in the same manner as in 8 above.

11. *Use of writing.* Average number of messages written, transmitted or received per participant. The period of reference may vary with the category of message, but should be averaged over one month. All written messages, with the exception of those submitted to the instructor, are taken into account (administrative notes, personal correspondence, forms filled in, etc.). All messages are of equal value as far as the indicator is concerned.

12. *Use of reading* (recommended indicator) [1]. One or other of the following sets of data should be utilized, according to circumstances: (a) Average number of written messages received (and read) per participant. The period of reference may vary with the category of message but should be adjusted to average one month. All written messages, with the exception of those emanating from the instructor, are taken into account (personal correspondence, administrative circulars, magazines, books, newspapers, etc.). All written messages are considered of equal value. (b) Average number, per inhabitant, of written

---

1. The third meeting of evaluation specialists of EWLP selected eleven 'minimum' and nineteen 'recommended' indicators.

messages arriving in the locality or region under consideration (procedure as above).
13. *Use of arithmetic* (recommended indicator). This indicator is of the same type as the two previous ones. Basic data will consist of evidence of calculations and measurements carried out by participants in the context of household accounting, accountancy in associations and co-operatives, etc.

Indicators of change

Economic growth and development indicators

14. Growth of output per inhabitant: percentage increase in the volume of production achieved through activities covered by the programme of training and in relation to output at the beginning of the programme. Data for this indicator may be gathered at different levels: community, group of communities, enterprises, factories or workshops, and/or at the level of groups of participants. The impact of literacy training may be assessed by reference to control groups or by any other suitable method.
15. Product quality (recommended indicator): changes in distribution of commercialized output by qualitative grades. In view of the variety of standards applied in different countries for quality control, it is impossible here to suggest a common indicator.
16. Sale price: this indicator may be calculated when the sale price of products actually reflects changes in the relationships between producers and the market. The figures to be compared must relate to identical quantities of products of equal quality.
17. Unit costs of production: in view of the variety of elements which might be taken into account, it is again not possible here to define a common indicator. However, wherever it is possible to identify a element in given conditions, the unit costs of production should be compared over a given period of time and/or between different production units, for such elements as insecticides, chemical fertilizers, accidents and absenteeism, purchase of materials, maintenance and repair of machinery, interest on loans, etc. Calculations for this type of indicator should be made on the basis of an entire community, of different sections of the community, or of individual enterprises, factories or workshops.

18. Changes in volume of durable goods and improvements which help to raise living standards. These changes are measured over a period of one year, on the basis of a previously established list of elements, and are expressed in percentages of increase.

    Assets in use and improvements effected which reflect technical changes might include: more efficient distance / time ratios (e.g. use of bicycles), better time-keeping (watches and alarm clocks), improved communication (radio sets), better conditions of storage and protection of goods (padlocks, locks and bolts), functional improvements in housing (construction of roofs, ventilation, lighting, etc.), improved water supply (wells, piped water, etc.) better protection against insects and parasites (mosquito nets, insecticides, etc.).

    The goods and improvements to be taken into account should be chosen from among those accessible to, and obtainable by, the populations concerned.
19. Changes in net global monetary income of individuals, measured in terms of percentage increases over incomes at the outset of the programme. The impact of functional literacy training may be assessed by reference to control groups or by any other suitable method. The indicator may be calculated for groups of participants, communities, workshops or enterprises.
20. Additions to equipment for production, maintenance and transport. This indicator is recommended for programmes involving small-scale producers and is measured in terms of the overall increase in the amount of such equipment, produced locally or elsewhere and acquired by individuals or communities for use by owners or others, averaged out over a period of several years.
21. Important changes in socio-economic attitudes and in the concept of the role of individuals in society. It is impossible to define a standard indicator in connection with this criterion; the components should be defined separately for each project, with reference to the exact social status of each participant.

Indicators concerning attitudes to education
22. Ratio of school attendance of participants' children: number of children of participants at school, over total number of children of school age. This ratio is calculated annually for each sex.
23. Ratio of wastage among participants' children: number of these children abandoning school, over number of school-age children

abandoning their studies in the population as a whole. This ratio is also calculated annually for each sex.

Indicators concerning vocational/occupational skills
24. Rate of adoption of innovations in production (recommended indicator); average number of innovations adopted per individual over the total number of innovations proposed in the programme in question.
25. Level of know-how in fields covered by the programme: percentage of successful candidates in one or more tests of practical know-how. Several successive tests count as one.
26. Growth in the desire for technical change and innovation (recommended indicator): relative number of expressions of desire for change and innovation in a certain number of fields defined at the outset of the programme.

Indicators concerning use of mass communication media
27. Use of radio and television sets: percentage of participants owning radio and/or television sets compared with the percentage of non-participants who own such means of information.
28. Interest shown in educational broadcasts (recommended indicator): average number of educational or technical broadcasts listened to or viewed, per participant.

Indicators concerning health, hygiene and safety
29. Acquisition of knowledge concerning health, hygiene and safety: this indicator, particularly intended for programmes designed for industrial workers, is measured in the same manner as 10 above.

Needless to say, this lengthy list of indicators is intended merely to provide examples from which each team will select only those which match its own objectives, concerns and capabilities. Nevertheless, in order to facilitate international comparison, each project should endeavour to retain, in the forms set out above, the basic statistical indicators concerning participation in programmes and the measurement of acquired skills.

B   Experimental and control groups

The methods of evaluation most frequently employed involve demonstration (hence comparison) and explanation (hence analysis) of anticipated changes (hence construction and verification of hypotheses). This entails the constitution of pairs of identical groups, the first of which serves for experimentation and the second for control. After formulating the hypothesis, the evaluator proceeds with the appropriate instruments to verify its reliability by investigating the changes which occur in the two groups and comparing them both before and after the experiment.

The two groups should thus be matched and similar in characteristics to the maximum possible extent, as entities if whole communities are the subject of investigation, or as individuals (age, sex, economic status, etc.) if the investigation concerns the participants in the project. The following example of the constitution of groups is taken from one of the EWLP projects, in which the 'concession'—as the smallest sociologically representative unit—was selected as the basic statistical unit.

The experimental plan

A selection of 64 villages in a cotton-growing sector of the project area, covering a total of 663 villages, was taken as a sample for the evaluation at the village level of expected sociological, economic and cultural changes. This sample included 32 out of the 269 villages eligible for experimental literacy training because they included at least one literate person capable of acting as an instructor, and 32 villages which did not meet this indispensable condition[1] and which were therefore to serve as the control group. The two groups of villages were matched with reference to two additional, external variables, 'cotton' and 'population', which were added to the experimental 'literacy' variable. This arrangement was intended, according to the author of the report on the project,[2] to permit 'choice between the hypothesis of convergence of variables and the hypothesis of interaction between factors'. A third external variable, 'language', was then introduced.

The four possible combinations of the first two external variables (P = population of the village; and C = degree of integration with the market economy as indicated by the average area of cotton cultivated per inhabitant) could then be expressed as follows:

1. It goes without saying that the momentary refusal to a community of the benefits of functional literacy training, and its relegation to the status of a control village, can only be justified by such a grave shortcoming.
2. Pierre Clément, Methodological introduction to *Comportements Socio-économiques et Modes de Vie en Région Cotonnière—Évaluation Initiale* (with Marianne Rupp). Bamako, Projet Pilote d'Alphabétisation Fonctionnelle du Mali, 1972. (In French only.)

Techniques and instruments

$C + P +$ = highly cultivated, densely populated (+ 5.15 ares[1] of cotton per inhabitant; + 324 inhabitants)
$C + P -$ = highly cultivated, thinly populated (+ 5.15 ares of cotton per inhabitant; — 271 inhabitants)
$C - P +$ = sparsely cultivated, densely populated (— 2.46 ares of cotton per inhabitant; + 324 inhabitants)
$C - P -$ = sparsely cultivated, thinly populated (— 2.46 ares of cotton per inhabitant; — 271 inhabitants).

Each of these groups (which comprised 8 villages each) was further divided into two sub-groups $L+$ and $L-$, depending upon whether or not the dominant mother tongue was the national language (in which the teaching was to be provided).[2] Wherever possible, the villages were selected by simple randon sampling from the groups corresponding to the different combinations of variables. Ten 'concessions' in each village were then selected by systematic sampling. The survey thus covered 64 villages and 634 families grouped into 'concessions'; it included a few villages comprising less than ten concessions for which there were no alternatives.

The experimental plan may be graphically represented thus:

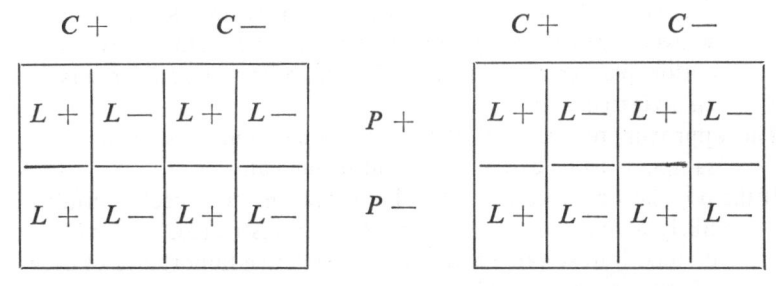

$C+$		$C-$			$C+$		$C-$	
$L+$	$L-$	$L+$	$L-$	$P+$	$L+$	$L-$	$L+$	$L-$
$L+$	$L-$	$L+$	$L-$	$P-$	$L+$	$L-$	$L+$	$L-$

Experimental sample   *Control sample*

Homogeneity of the sample

The experimental and control villages were matched as closely as possible. However, in order to enhance the demonstrative value of the

1. 1 are = 100 m² or 119.6 square yards.
2. In actual fact, there were four modes of the variable 'language' and not two, and the experiment as first planned was more complex than it appears here. But a plan containing three two-way external variables is sufficiently difficult to conduct under field conditions (and two are frequently a maximum when working with 'natural' groups), so that the above presentation was judged adequate.

expected results, data relevant to indicators likely to be used during the experiment were gathered during the preliminary survey in the 64 villages and 634 concessions concerned, and then subjected to variance analysis in order to test the homogeneity of the samples relating to each indicator, on the basis of an assumption that the experimental and control groups would be similar with respect to variables in which modifications were hoped for as the result of literacy action. In the absence of significant differences between the two groups, the indicator in question was retained; when the contrary was the case, a specific decision was taken with regard to its rejection, replacement or retention.

C Samples

The construction of samples was a weak point in the surveys conducted by the EWLP evaluation teams. It may therefore be useful to set out below some of the basic rules which should be observed if samples are to prove reliable.

The statistical unit of the survey should be defined with the maximum precision. Examples: 'mining face-workers; spinners and weavers aged between 15 and 45 in specific factories; wives of cotton planters; unskilled building workers; small farmers in an irrigated area'; etc.

The approximative size of the entire population from which the sample is to be extracted should be indicated.

If the population concerned is not homogeneous in respect of criteria likely to influence the variable to be investigated, it should be divided into suitable strata, and the relative importance of each of these strata should be calculated.

An adequate degree of precision for the formulation of results should be determined.

Limits of reliability of the sample should be determined.

Tables of reference indicating the size of the sample to be used, taking account of the overall population concerned, the degree of precision of the survey and the reliability limits of the sample, should be consulted.

The size of the sample should be weighted according to the coefficient of mortality adopted.

The sample should be distributed over the different strata of the population concerned.

The elements of the sample should be selected by random sampling in each of the strata.

Each evaluation report should include a brief introductory methodological chapter clearly indicating how the sample was constructed, what adjustments were necessary, what modifications of the experimental plan were required to adapt it to on-the-spot realities, the difficulties encountered and—in general—the degree of reliability which can be attributed to the results of the survey. Thus, eventual users of the data will be able to evaluate the inherent risks and uncertainties, and decide whether to retain the results for further study or to reject them.

5 Analysis of results

Having examined the most suitable instruments and techniques for the evaluation of literacy programmes, we must now study the most commonly used methods of analysis. The task of the evaluator is above all to describe, to compare and to explain—or rather to attempt to provide an explanation.

Description, comparison, explanation

Descriptive studies. The importance of surveys of the milieu and of descriptive statistical tables has been indicated above (Section 3). These provide sufficient evidence, after study, to identify the categories of participants or instructors and the groups or programmes in which literacy action appears to be making progress or to be falling behind. Simple percentage calculations will permit, for example, early identification of the most assiduous participants, of those who drop out, of those who are obtaining the best results, in which regions, with which instructors, in which programmes, etc.

Such studies, numerous examples of which will be found in the specialized chapters which follow, will permit a certain measure of classification of the groups concerned, although it will not be possible to determine with certainty whether the differences between them are significant. Yet they are of a revelational nature and may permit certain pedagogical or institutional adjustments.

Comparative studies. The most interesting of these are developmental or 'process' studies, which make it possible to calculate from a single table to what extent there has been progress or regression, to determine whether certain results differ positively or negatively from others, and whether the difference is significant. Simple statistical tests, applied to the processing of the data, will provide a wealth of material for purposes of comparison of averages, frequencies and variances and for identification of links through study of correlation coefficients, etc.

Analytical studies. Proceeding from description and synchronic or diachronic comparison, the next stage, namely analysis and research designed to provide explanations, is important in internal and external evaluation alike. On the basis of simple hypotheses or explanatory theoretical models, the evaluator will endeavour to understand the phenomena observed, to determine the relative importance of different inputs to the final results and, if possible, to propose modifications designed either to improve the existing situation (by mid-course correction or feedback) or to introduce new action based on observation of models.

More often than not, these analytical studies will be based on the examination of variations observed with regard to different indicators and on attempts to detect possible relationships between them. The following procedures might be employed: construction of an explanatory theoretical model; division of the model into basic hypotheses; subdivision of these hypotheses into simple assumptions involving a limited number of indicators with easily defined variations (with/without; before/after; inter/intra; etc.); application of suitable statistical measurements for validation or invalidation of the hypotheses.

Hypotheses

How is a hypothesis constructed and verified? Let us return to the example given in the introduction to this guide concerning the launching of a project designed to render a certain number of women in a given region literate, by means of teaching which will involve the use of radio. Suppose we wish to determine whether teaching by radio is a worth-while proposition and, if so, with which categories of participants. Our hypothesis may be formulated as follows: 'Teaching is more effective when it is accompanied by radio broadcasts on the same subject.'

The task of the evaluator will be to devise various procedures by which this hypothesis may be verified, and to select those which are best suited to the situation, which are the simplest, the least costly, the most rapid, etc. Possibilities might include:
Comparison of the results of end-of-cycle tests in centres where the broadcasts have or have not been heard. This procedure involves the construction of matched samples, the calculation

of average success rates in tests, differences between averages, etc.

Construction of a test based on the material taught by radio, and application of the test under identical conditions to two groups of participants (control sample and experimental sample).

Construction of two tests of knowledge acquired—one concerning a subject taught by radio during a given week (food hygiene, for example), and the other concerning a subject taught solely by the instructor (e.g. child hygiene)—and application of the two tests to the same participants, who have all listened to the broadcasts, one week later and again two months later. This will permit investigation of the retention of knowledge taught with, and without, the assistance of radio.

Distribution of a questionnaire inviting participants to comment on the broadcasts: difficulties of understanding, interest value, duration, timing, frequency, etc., and subsequent analysis of the replies.

The evaluator may extend the statistical analysis still further with the aim of determining which category of women benefit most from the broadcasts: the younger or the older, the married or the unmarried, wage earners or those who have no paid employment, etc. For this purpose the groups to be tested will be constituted according to the selected characteristics, a list of which will be found below (Chapter IV, Section 3). The results of the tests will determine whether it is necessary to improve the broadcasts, to transmit the programmes more or less frequently, to extend them to a wider audience or to abandon them, etc.

The Appendix to this guide contains a number of hypotheses formulated during the global evaluation of EWLP, and the list may serve as a sound basis for selection. They are, however, included merely as examples, and the evaluator should not feel bound to adhere strictly to their present formulation.

Preliminary studies III

In the following pages we propose to describe, for each type of evaluation (see Chapter I, Section 1), the objectives involved, the fields covered, the instruments employed (with one or two frameworks which may serve as models); and to provide examples of the descriptive, comparative or explanatory studies which could be undertaken on the basis of the data collected.

1 Objectives and scope

Before evaluating the results of a literacy project, the evaluator's first task must be to assemble all the elements of information concerning participants and their environment which were necessary if the literacy action is to be undertaken without risk. These preliminary studies are required for experimental and operational programmes alike, and should be mainly concerned with: the explicit definition of the objectives of the project; the feasibility of the literacy action envisaged; the study of the milieu; the investigation of problems faced by the intended participants which, taken together, will furnish the subject-matter of the teaching to be provided.

It is at this stage of its activities that the evaluation team will complete the planning of its work.

2 Definition of objectives[1]

The evaluation of a project has two fixed points of reference: a point of departure determined by the initial social, economic and cultural situation of the prospective participants in their natural milieu; and a point of completion, i.e. the ultimate situation as conceived and desired by the authorities responsible for deciding on literacy action. The purpose of the evaluation will be to measure on the one hand the area covered between the point of departure and the point of arrival or termination of the project and, on the other hand, the positive or negative distance which may well separate the actual point of arrival from the point of completion. These calculations will make it possible to determine the extent to which the goal fixed by the political authorities has been attained.

To succeed in this task, the evaluator must resolutely eschew every definition of goals or objectives which is formulated in general terms such as 'eradication of illiteracy', 'completion of the literacy campaign', 'the promotion of women through education', 'the enhancement of economic growth through literacy', etc. Objectives must be defined precisely—and where possible quantitatively—in the shape of replies to such questions as: 'Who? How many? Where? When? How? Why?'

The required degree of precision may be obtained through discussion (at the highest possible level of responsibility) with political and administrative authorities at the governmental or ministerial level, with the development body to which the literacy project is attached or subordinated, and with the national services directly responsible for the project.

When all the objectives have been very explicitly defined, they are incorporated in a 'plan of operations', which should, ideally, be jointly signed by representatives of the three authorities mentioned above, and in which the objectives are related directly and specifically to the project, if possible with reference to the goals set out in national plans and/or in the plans of bodies concerned with economic or social development.

During this process, it will be very useful to assemble all the information which has served in the determination of the objectives: studies of various kinds, statistics, etc. (see Chapter II, Section 2). This information should deal with:

(i) The *region* concerned, whether geographical (plain, town,

---

1. For further details, see *Evaluation Globale du PEMA* (Document Technique II), *Le Cadre Institutionnel des Projets Expérimentaux*, Unesco, 1975. (In French only.)

etc.) or administrative (governorate, prefecture, district). Number of villages; area; etc.

(ii) The *populations* concerned: women, men, adolescents, children; salaried workers, industrial workers, craftsmen, foremen, farmers due to change their occupation, independent or salaried farm workers, unemployed youths, etc.; wives of agricultural or industrial workers, housewives and mothers, pregnant women, employees in industrial or handicraft workshops, etc. In all cases add age and numbers (actual or as a percentage of the total population).

(iii) *Target enterprises:* large independent or co-operative agricultural estates; small agricultural holdings affected by land reform or agricultural extension programmes; small mixed farms or large single-crop estates in an irrigated area; subsistence farming in an area of agricultural colonization; large-scale industrial construction enterprises, small-scale industries affected by development planning or by vocational training programmes; industrial zones, etc.; cottage industry, rural or tourist handicrafts, etc.

(iv) *Specific economic and/or social objectives:* attempts should be made, wherever possible, to quantify these objectives, for example, in agriculture: increased output (by how much, which process, which product), improvement of product quality, adoption of new techniques or materials (which); modification of working methods or conditions of production, increased diversification of production, etc.; in crafts and industry: increased output, improvement of product quality, increased productivity, improved hygiene and security, pre-vocational apprenticeship, etc.; in the social field: transformation of domestic living and working conditions, of attitudes; improvement of hygiene, health, child nutrition, etc.

(v) The *period:* planned date of commencement of the literacy action, planned duration; annual rhythm, etc., if possible with reference to development plans.

(vi) *The agreed concept of literacy action:* the type of literacy action envisaged should be clearly defined, by determining whether the aim is: merely to teach a large and non-specific population to read, write and count; firstly to teach reading, writing and arithmetic to a population directly involved in a development project which also intends to provide vocational or social training; firstly to provide vocational and/or social training, accompanied at all stages by literacy training.

Similarly the meanings attached in the project to 'illiterate', 'semi-literate', 'new literate' and 'post-literacy training' should be defined in very precise terms at the outset.

(vii) The *authority responsible for verifying* (in the medium or long term) whether the immediate objectives of the literacy training (as reflected in the programmes, teaching materials, etc.) coincide with the general objectives assigned to the project. This authority might take the form of a 'national literacy committee', jointly composed of representatives of the government or ministries, representatives of the development body to which the project is attached, representatives of the authorities responsible for the project, and representatives of the project team itself.

3 Feasibility

The essential task here is to provide those responsible for the project with the elements required for taking a decision with regard to the launching of literacy action, either in a specific area or with a specific category of participants. Studies should cover the following points:

(i) The *political will* to encourage or support literacy action with the aim of transforming the milieu. It should be determined whether this political will is manifest at all levels (central, regional, local) and reflected, for example, in statements and speeches concerning literacy by members of the government, and whether it is reflected in a definite juridical form through the adoption of laws, decrees, orders, governmental decisions, ministerial circulars, by-laws, etc. The nature and importance of governmental and non-governmental support (other than financial or administrative) should also be determined, together with the rank of the project director in the administrative hierarchy and the arrangements made for liaison with the development body concerned. Finally, the degree of participation by non-governmental organizations—trade unions, women's organizations, student bodies, etc.—and by political parties should be established.

(ii) *Project autonomy.* A project which is entirely autonomous and independent of any ministry or economic organization is unlikely to survive for very long. Autonomy in respect of the actual literacy action is important, but there should be close liaison with a ministry on the one hand, and with a development scheme on the other. It will then be necessary to determine the degree of integration of the project both with the sponsoring ministry and with the development body of which it may well be a component. This will involve the preparation of an organizational chart showing the importance and the nature of the administrative and managerial links established between the three parties. Awareness of the extent to which the project is autonomous on the one hand, and integrated on the other, will permit the identification of possible sources of conflit (with regard *inter alia* to authority) or contradiction, and to ensure rationality by determining, for example, whether the planned framework of the project will permit its evolution in conformity with the methodological, logical and chronological imperatives of functional literacy.

(iii) *Adequacy of financial and material resources.* This involves determining whether the timing of support matches the requirements of the project plan, whether sufficient budgetary provision has been made by the sponsoring ministry, and whether material and financial support will be forthcoming from the development organization concerned throughout the duration of the project (provision of premises, transportation, instructors, overtime, leave of absence from work to attend courses, etc).

(iv) *Human resources.* Are the necessary human resources available locally? Docs the anticipated administrative support exist at the local and regional levels? Are there enough local instructors? Will support be forthcoming from local populations and their leading personalities, for example, in the provision of voluntary labour for the construction of a classroom, or the creation of a local literacy committee?

(v) *Motivation surveys.* These have a twofold objective: In the first place they should permit identification of the villages or town-sectors the inhabitants of which are favourable to literacy action; of the motivations which incline them to favour development; of the advantages which they expect to gain from the ability to read and write; and of the difficulties which they expect to encounter during the learning process.

Secondly, they should endeavour to enlist the support of the villagers themselves in the elaboration of the programme of functional literacy training. The programme may, in fact, be designed starting from either of two points of departure: the first is the planning as conceived by those responsible for the economic and social development of the region concerned, which determines the transformations they wish to effect in the mentality, life-styles and working habits of the population, treating the individual peasant essentially as a specimen of *homo economicus*; the second is the personality of the subject-individual himself, as expressed in his desires, doubts, difficulties and current needs. The addition to a literacy programme, as a matter of priority, of some or all of the villagers' own demands for knowledge has a humanizing effect, and links the programme more closely to the peasant than to the technician.

The motivation survey is conducted either through interviews with a sample of the prospective participants or through open meetings in regions where the inhabitants are accustomed to expressing themselves in public. But to avoid encountering inhibitions or reticences due to sex, age or social status, these gatherings should be homogeneous and confined in turn to leading personalities, men, women, and finally the younger generation.

The investigation or interviews should be centred on the following questions:

Why do the people wish to learn to read, write and count?

What do they wish to learn, in addition to reading, writing and arithmetic?

What benefits do they expect from literacy?

In what circumstances have they felt inferior as a result of being illiterate?

Do they believe that it is difficult to learn?

Does their environment include factors that may obstruct their will to become literate?

The replies to these questions should be analysed according to sex, age group and social category, and the survey should be completed by an investigation of the extent to which the local administrative authorities and those responsible for development favour or oppose literacy training.

(vi) *Investigation of the milieu.* The task here is to collect, for each village, community or urban district, the information which will permit firstly the creation of an 'identity card' for each community and, secondly, the selection of the indicators to be used in the baseline survey at the outset of the project. This will permit selection of those villages where literacy training is to be provided (experimental groups) and those to be used for purposes of comparison (matched control groups: see Chapter II, Section 4). Chapter II, Section 3, contains the outline of a survey which might be used for this investigation of the milieu.

Information will be collected by direct observation, or from the local authorities or from the technicians in the fields. The personal characteristics of the inhabitants may be investigated by sampling among individuals or, better still, among households each member of which over the age of 15 will be questioned and at the same time subjected to the 'literacy scale' test (see Appendix, Document 5). Lastly, in the case of agricultural programmes, note should be taken of each type of crop cultivated or gathered, of the different stages of development of the species concerned and of the main labours involved, in order to draw up an agricultural calendar which should indicate:

Sequence, dates and duration of plant-growth phenomena.

Sequence, importance, intensity, dates and duration of agricultural activities.
Sequence, importance, intensity, dates and duration of non-agricultural rural activities.

The collection of all the above information will make it possible to advance a reasonable hypothesis concerning the feasibility or non-feasibility of the project both as a whole and in specific areas or environments. The likelihood of success of literacy action in each of the communities concerned should be assessed by reference to the favourable elements so identified, such as: the existence of authentic and deep-rooted motivation; the weight given to requests for knowledge in different economic and social fields; the existence of potential literacy teachers (numbers, names and level of education); the existence of an organized village structure; the possibility of obtaining premises for the courses; the existence of communication facilities; the existence of a supporting infrastructure; the support of local authorities and/or technicians; willingness to collaborate on the part of the authorities and of local development bodies; etc.

Also by reference to such unfavourable elements as: an excessively high ratio of illiterates; inadequacy or non-existence of a rural community consciousness; poor conditions of health and nutrition; difficulty of access, inadequate or non-existent infrastructure; absence of incentives to development; opposition of influential personalities; excessively strong or numerous taboos; hostility of the population towards change; etc.

4 Identification of programme content

By now, the evaluator will have: (a) defined with precision the objectives to be attained (this knowledge will be vital when he comes to draw up a balance-sheet of the literacy action), and (b), as a result of the feasibility study, a relatively exact notion of the chances of success of the operation, either as a whole or with regard to specific areas or populations. All these studies will also furnish the other project teams (responsible for direction, instruction and methodology) with indispensable information. It now remains to list the 'problems' faced by the population concerned or by the technicians in charge of development, the solution of which will permit the individuals involved to improve their patterns and standards of living and to become 'effective agents in the process of socio-economic development'.[1] The investigation of these problems and obstacles

---

1. cf. 'The Central Hypothesis of Functional Literacy', in Chapter I.

will make it possible to draw up the programmes of functional literacy training, and as this is a matter of direct concern to the methodologists, it is in close collaboration with them that the exercise should be conducted.

The literacy programme

On the basis of the specific objectives defined as a result of the studies mentioned in Section 2 above, the methodologists will formulate a variety of programmes designed to meet the particular requirements of:

A clearly defined geographical area: urban or rural, savannah, forest, coastal or lakeside, irrigated plain, etc.

An administrative area (province, district, etc.).

A specific cultural area (linguistic, ethnic).

A specific economic or social sector (rural, industrial, unemployed persons, women, etc.).

General vocational training (all-round education, industrial problems, promotion of women, etc.).

Well-defined professional training (weaving, mechanics, cotton-growing, etc.).

Highly diversified professional upgrading (improvement of rice cultivation, maintenance of machinery, child care, etc.).

If necessary, the situations listed above may be combined. Different programmes may be conceived in a variety of forms:

As totally distinct, according to the vocational training envisaged and the geographical, administrative or cultural area concerned, but structured in 'modules' (short groups of sequences dealing with the same subject) which can be transferred from one programme to another.

As distinct entities in the same manner as above, but without a modular structure.

As sharing a common stem, but with specific sequences for each type of training envisaged.

As absolutely identical, irrespective of the area and population involved and of the occupations of the participants.

The above list is given in order of preference, since it reflects the degree of functional concentration of the programmes to be formulated for the project.

Problem definition

The evaluation unit's contribution to the formulation of these programmes will comprise a series of surveys and studies carried out with the appropriate administrative and professional authorities

Preliminary studies

and with the population groups concerned. This work will take the following directions:

(i) The identification by prospective participants of the problems they encounter and the changes of life-style which they desire; and the application to these prospective participants of tests which will permit the creation of an inventory of the intellectual and technical aptitudes of the whole population concerned.

(ii) The preparation by the foremen, technicians, engineers and managers responsible for economic and social development (in agriculture, industry, crafts, etc.) of lists of technical, professional, social, economic or other problems which obstruct the desired process of development, and which may include:

Lack of intellectual abilities: reading, writing, counting, measurement, calculation of areas or percentages, interpretation of sketches, diagrams, etc. These shortcomings should be described in the greatest possible detail.

Lack of professional skills: ability to operate or adjust a machine, etc.

Lack of conscientiousness: absenteeism, etc.

Neglect of safety regulations.

Lack of know-how.

Difficulties or hostility with regard to the adoption, for example in agriculture, of new techniques (irrigation, fertilizers, double-cropping, etc.) or products (high-yield varieties, etc.).

Anti-progressive attitudes and behaviour.

Etc.

(iii) Indications by the various regional administrators, technicians or specialists (doctors, health workers, veterinary surgeons, welfare officers, agricultural advisers, child educationists, factory inspectors, etc.) of the modifications in life-style of which they wish to see the emergence among illiterates and which reflect governmental decisions concerning the economic and/or social development of the populations concerned.

Most of the above information may be derived from the preliminary studies already completed in the form of: discussion with the responsible administrative and technical authorities; investigation of the milieu, observations *in situ;* technical monographs; motivation survey; results of 'literacy scale' tests; scrutiny of documentation so far gathered.

Problem listing

The next stage involves the classification, under major headings, of all the elements listed, in the order of priority given on the one hand by the participants and on the other by the technicians. This may well result in opposite points of view among those concerned, for example, with regard to the speed of production ('cadences') in workshops. Obstacles of which the origins lie in the environment will be distinguished from those attributable to lack of ability or to negative attitudes of individuals. This classification has the merit of providing the methodologists with a detailed catalogue which should permit the elaboration of programmes likely to help the participants to take various forms of action such as the following:

To transform their environment: by improving their housing (waterproofing, combating cold or heat, installing kitchens, opening windows, etc.); by making their homes more healthy (burning rubbish, building lavatories, combating mosquitoes, etc.); by improving their surroundings (constructing hen-runs, making vegetable gardens, planting trees, cutting back weeds and so discouraging snakes, etc.); by improving the quality of their water supply (controlling springs and wells, using filters); etc.

To acquire knowledge and skills: of an instrumental nature (reading, writing, counting, calculating); of a technical or vocational nature; of a medical, hygienic or nutritional nature; of a cultural, historical, geographical or social nature; of a scientific nature; of a political, civic or syndicalist nature; of an economic nature (production, productivity, income, standard of living, etc.); etc.

To modify their attitudes through: the elimination of taboos and superstitions; the removal of reticence with regard to technology and technological innovation; the adoption of new patterns of behaviour with regard to the education of children, hygiene, family planning, etc.; the development of aspirations towards better living and the improvement of their own and their children's professional qualifications; an increased interest and more active participation in the functioning of the society to which they belong; etc.

By now the methodologist will have at his disposal, for the elaboration of the curricula of the literacy programmes, the following elements of information collected by the evaluation team:

The results of studies on the specificity of the objectives assigned to the project.

The results of investigations of the milieu.

The results of motivation surveys.

The results of studies concerned with the identification of problems.

The results of studies concerning the aptitudes required of participants.

The results of studies concerning the intellectual and technical aptitudes of the participants.

At this point the methodologist's task is to classify, with reference to the orders of priority given by the various persons questioned, the problems in the order in which they are to be solved during the learning process. He must consequently endeavour to harmonize:
The economic requirements of the bodies responsible for development.
The social imperatives of the socio-professional situations involved.
The pedagogical demands of the different disciplines to be taught.
Priority of a suitable degree will be given to one or other of these elements according to circumstances.

5 Action planning

We have seen that the evaluator's action is extremely varied and complex, that it is integrated and that it also has an integrating function. Based on observation and comparison, this action must develop in such a way that the two processes are kept closely in line. For this reason, it must necessarily be planned with due regard to logistical and pedagogical imperatives. It is no less indispensable for the evaluator's colleagues to respect certain of the methodological imperatives of evaluation—particularly those which relate to its scientific aspects, and first and foremost to the establishment and preservation of autonomous variables. Accordingly there should be constant and far-reaching concertation between the methodologists and the evaluators.

At the outset the evaluator should draw up a detailed workplan and submit it to his partners in the project, with the aim of obtaining not only their criticisms and suggestions for amendment, but also the assurance that they will help him to remain within the limits of the plan.

Figure 1 sets out in schematic form the different stages of planning for the evaluation of a functional literacy programme. Only the most important stages are included, and no indication is given of the time-lapse between each, since this will depend on individual situations.

Key to the stages of the plan

(a) Preliminary studies

1. Appointment of the person responsible for the evaluation unit.
2. Recruitment of the members of the unit.

The evaluation of literacy programmes

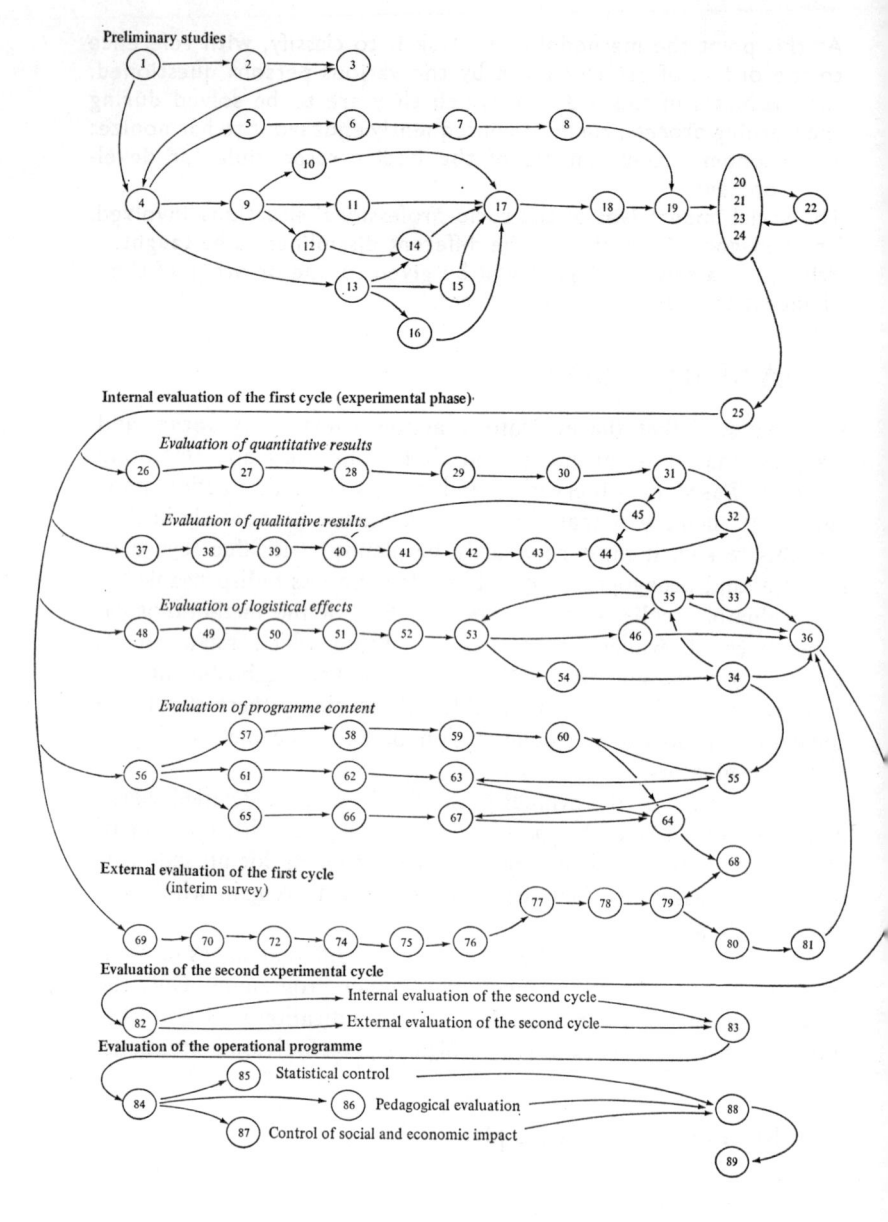

FIG. 1. Stages in planning for the evaluation of a functional literacy programme.

Preliminary studies

3. Training of team members.
4. Planning of preliminary studies.
5. Planning of the study concerning the definition of objectives.
6. Collection of the necessary documentation.
7. Discussions in connection with the definition of objectives.
8. Drafting of conclusions of the study on objectives.
9. Planning of the feasibility study.
10. Discussions with political authorities.
11. Discussions with development organizations.
12. Discussions with representatives of non-governmental organizations.
13. Planning of the study of the milieu.
14. Start of motivation survey.
15. Start of field survey of communities.
16. Start of 'literacy scale' study.
17. Drafting of the conclusions of the study of the milieu.
18. Publication of the results of the objectives survey.
19. Drafting of the conclusions of the feasibility study.
20. Selection of areas and populations to be covered.
21. Elaboration of curriculum.
22. Construction of weekly and end-of-cycle tests.
23. Training of instructors.
24. Enlistment of participants and constitution of groups.

(b) Internal evaluation of the first cycle (experimental phase)

(i) *Evaluation of quantitative results*

25. Construction of the experimental plan for the first cycle of literacy training.
26. Preparation of the plan for the evaluation of quantitative results.
27. Formulation of the hypotheses to be verified and construction of tables of data to be collected.
28. Selection of criteria.
29. Selection and preparation of indicators.
30. Determination of the periodicity of measurements.
31. Preparation of the instruments of measurement and exprimentation.
32. Periodical statistical measurement.
33. Data collection and study, first at the regional level and then at project headquarters.
34. Publication of statistical tables.
35. Detailed studies of quantitative results.
36. Feedback action on programme implementation.

(ii) *Evaluation of qualitative results*

37. Preparation of the plan for the evaluation of qualitative fesults.
38. Formulation of the hypotheses to be verified and construction of tables of data to be collected.
39. Selection of criteria.
40. Selection and preparation of indicators.
41. Preparation of instruments of measurement.

42. Construction and try-out of tests.
43. Determination of the periodicity of measurements.
44. Preparation of sample studies.
45. Selection of samples for random tests.
46. Detailed studies of qualitative results.
(32.)
(33.) } Feedback action on programme implementation.
(34.)
(36.)

(iii) *Evaluation of logistical impact*

48. Preparation of plan for evaluation of the impact of logistic components of the project: list of tables to be prepared and hypotheses to be verified.
49. Selection and preparation of criteria and indicators.
50. Selection of samples for random tests.
51. Preparation of instruments and collection of data.
52. Publication of statistical tables and descriptive studies.
53. Correlation with data from the studies of quantitative and qualitative results.
54. Detailed studies of results of evaluation of the logistic components of the programme.
(34.) (After publication of statistical tables:)
(36.) Feedback action on programme implementation.

(iv) *Evaluation of programme content*

56. Preparation of plan for evaluation of programme content.
57. Formulation of hypotheses to be verified concerning adequacy of programme content with regard to the objectives of the project and to the populations concerned.
58. Construction of questionnaires to be used for expert judgement.
59. Start of surveys in connection with expert judgements.
60. Publication of results and correlation with the results of the internal evaluation.
61. Formulation of hypotheses to be verified concerning evolution of the programme.
62. Collection of data and publication of results.
63. Correlation with results of evaluation of quantitative and qualitative results.
55. Publication of explanatory studies concerning quantitative and qualitative results, logistical impact and evolution of the programme.
65. Formulation of hypotheses concerning pedagogical principles of functional literacy and methods and materials employed.
66. Selection of samples and miscellaneous tests.
67. Publication of the results of tests and correlation with the results of earlier experiments.
64. Publication of results of experiments concerning the evaluation of programme content.
(36.) Feedback action on programme implementation.

Preliminary studies

68. Synthesis of results of internal evaluation of the first cycle.

(c) External evaluation of the first cycle (interim survey)

69. Construction of overall plan for external evaluation of the first cycle (interim survey).
For each of the main fields covered by external evaluation:
70. Formulation of hypotheses to be verified.
71. Selection of criteria, indicators, indices.
72. Constitution of experimental and control groups.
73. Preparation of instruments. Determination of periodicity of measurements.
74. Initial measurements.
75. Periodical measurements.
76. Final measurements of the interim phase.
77. Publication of statistical tables and descriptive studies.
78. Comparative studies.
79. Correlation with results of internal evaluation.
80. Publication of results concerning the verification of hypotheses.
81. Feedback action on the elaboration of the programme for the first cycle.

(d) Evaluation of the second experimental cycle

82. Construction of overall plan for internal and external evaluation of the second cycle, which may be conducted as for first cycle.
83. Publication of results of the evaluation of the experimental programme, and decisions with regard to preparation and implementation of operational programme.

(e) Evaluation of the operational programme

84. Construction of the overall plan for the evaluation of the operational programme.
88. Publication of results, cycle by cycle and stage by stage, of the evaluation of the programme.
89. Feedback action on programme implementation.

Quantitative evaluation of results IV

1 Objectives

The initial purpose of measuring the quantitative results of literacy training is to furnish those responsible for the project with a quantified description of its activities. The instruments of measurement will be designed to permit the systematic collection from each work unit of adequate data to be used for comparisons between periods, or between groups, or within groups. The tasks of the evaluation team will therefore involve the analysis of these results in order to determine what improvements can be made in the system so that the quantitative returns from literacy courses may provide the maximum yield.

2 Scope

The essential need is to collect from each course a certain amount of information concerning:

The participants: Registers of participants are kept by group, containing, for each individual, details of: sex; age; marital status; number of children (and number attending school); occupation and if possible professional status, i.e. level of qualification, relationship with the land cultivated (owner, farmer, tenant); level of literacy (see Appendix, Document 5); language normally spoken.

Attendance: A monthly register of attendance (see Appendix, Documents 1 and 2) is brought up to date daily, and permits monthly calculations of the number of sessions held, the total number of absences by sex, age group and cause of absence, and the ratio of absenteeism. This register, like the register of participants, is analysed at the local level.

Progress of courses: A monthly report (see Appendix, Document 2) is transmitted to the regional authorities at the end of each month for processing. This report contains the overall statistics from the monthly register (Document 1), together with information concerning supervisors' visits, the teaching material received and current expenditure, as well as the instructor's report on teaching activities and the results of weekly or monthly tests.

End-of-cycle examinations: An end-of-cycle report (see Appendix, Document 3) will indicate success-rates with regard both to the batch and to the number of participants in the cycle concerned, and also provide end-of-cycle statistics. This document is analysed and processed at the regional level and at project headquarters.

Instructors and supervisors: Individual records, kept for each instructor and supervisor, indicate: sex; age; socio-professional origins (literate peasant, teacher, agricultural extension worker, foreman, etc.); level of education; teaching qualifications; training courses attended; seniority. These records are analysed at the regional level and at project headquarters.

All the above-mentioned documents will be utilized for both operational and experimental programmes.

3 Descriptive studies

The first task is to identify the participants. This involves the summation of data concerning the participants in each course by geographical or administrative area, instructional technology, supervisory body (ministry, semi-official or non-governmental organization, etc.). Composite tables are drawn up on the basis of the main characteristics of the participants, and these statistics will be made available at the local and regional levels and at project headquarters.

1-1 Participants by sex and age group.
1-2 Participants by marital status, number of children and number of children attending school.
1-3 Participants by occupation and qualifications and/or socio-economic status (relationship to the land, area cultivated, etc., for farmers).

Quantitative evaluation of results

1-4 Participants by language normally spoken and level of education.

The next task is to identify drop-outs. Further tables may be drawn up on the basis of principal characteristics of participants and instructors, e.g.

1-5 Drop-outs by sex and age group.
1-6 Drop-outs by marital status, number of children and number of children attending school.
1-7 Drop-outs by occupation (see 1-3 above).
1-8 Drop-outs by language normally spoken and level of education;
1-9 Drop-outs by ascertained cause.
1-10 Drop-outs by age and sex of instructor.
1-11 Drop-outs by socio-professional origins of instructor (same origins as participant, government official, volunteer, etc.).
1-12 Drop-outs by professional qualifications of instructor (number of training courses attended, seniority, etc.).
1-13 Drop-outs by level of education of instructor.
1-14 Drop-outs by average number of monthly group sessions.
1-15 Drop-outs after 1, 2, 3, 4, etc., months of literacy training.

Attempts may also be made to determine who is frequently absent and why. New tables may be drawn up on the basis of the characteristics of the participants and instructors, and of ratios of absenteeism, to be numbered 1-16 to 1-26 and to cover the variables listed in 1-5 to 1-15 above.

Taken together, these tables will indicate who abandons courses or is frequently absent, when, why and where. The tables will also permit the calculation of basic statistical indicators of participation in courses (see Chapter II, Section 4), while comparison of these data with statistics collected during the baseline survey will permit calculation of the ratio of coverage (Indicator 5); it will also be possible to calculate for each month the ratio of registration for a given programme (Indicator 1), the ratio of drop-outs (Indicator 2), the ratio of attendance (Indicator 3), the ratio of time-utilization (Indicator 4) and—at the end of a programme or cycle—the ratio of participation in the final test (Indicator 6), the participants/instructor ratio, etc.

4 Comparative studies

The purpose of these studies is first to permit the evaluation of the progress made by different groups (diachronic studies), then to identify those groups whose performance is significantly above or below the average and, ultimately, to define the characteristics of individuals whose performance differs significantly from the norm (comparisons within and between groups).

Calculation of the month-by-month evolution of indicators concerning attendance, drop-outs and number of sessions held should make it possible to determine whether, for example, registrations, drop-outs, absenteeism and a decline in the number of sessions held are more pronounced in certain months than in others (investigation of statistical differences).

The ratios for individual groups may also be compared monthly with the overall average, thus making it possible to identify by region, by sponsoring body or by instructional technology the groups whose performance is significantly above or below average. Further study of the characteristics of groups (size, situation, homogeneity), participants or instructors may make it possible to determine likely causes of discrepancies.

5 Explanatory studies

The descriptive or comparative studies mentioned above will frequently suffice for the identification of favourable or unfavourable situations, whether specific or general, and their essential causes, so that remedial action may be taken at the level of those causes with the aim of improving attendance at courses.

Moreover, the data furnished by these studies may permit project leaders who so desire but whose resources are limited to extend the investigation progressively; for example, to determine whether two or more series of variables are related to each other and to what extent, or to verify some of the hypotheses set out in the Appendix to this guide (Document 8) or other hypotheses of their own making.

The influences which affect absenteeism and drop-out and which modify the relevant ratios may be investigated by the application of complex methods of analysis (e.g. Wroclaw's taxonomic analysis) to theoretical models, but also through the verification of simple hypotheses with the aid of statistical tests which are easier to manipulate (difference of averages or frequencies, variance analysis, calculation of correlation coefficients, multiple correlation, co-variants, factorial analysis.

Attempts might be made, for example, to determine:
Whether drop-out, absenteeism and participation in examinations are interrelated. One hypothesis might be that drop-out and absenteeism have the same origin, are two aspects of an identical phenomenon so that one may determine the other.

Quantitative evaluation of results

Another hypothesis might be that drop-out and absenteeism have an influence on participation in examinations and that high rates for the former lead to low, or high, rates for the latter.

Whether registration, drop-out, absenteeism, participation and success in examinations are collectively or individually related to certain personal characteristics of participants such as sex, age, marital status, number of children, number of children attending school, professional qualifications, ownership or non-ownership of land, language normally spoken, etc.

Whether drop-out, absenteeism and participation in examinations are related to certain personal characteristics of instructors such as sex, age, level of previous training, teaching experience, literacy teaching experience, number of training courses attended, socio-economic origins, etc.

Whether drop-out, absenteeism and participation in examinations are related to participant/instructor ratios.

Whether drop-out, absenteeism and participation in examinations are related to the organization of groups (time-tables, premises, regions, lack of teaching materials, absence of supervision, delays in the evolution of the programme, number of sessions held, etc.).

Whether drop-out and absenteeism are related to the degree of success in earlier periods or cycles of literacy training; in other words, whether successful termination of the first cycle has a favourable influence on attendance during the second cycle, or whether success in examinations acts as an incentive.

Whether drop-out and absenteeism were predictable. This might involve the investigation of possible correspondences with unfavourable elements (lack of political will, for example) detected during the feasibility and motivation surveys and the investigation of the milieu (cf. Chapter III, Section 3 (vi)).

Whether drop-out and absenteeism are related to certain aspects of the methods and means of literacy training.

Whether drop-out and absenteeism are related to aspects of the institutional framework of the project such as: degree of integration with the political environment, degree of autonomy of the project, degree of integration with different institutions, state of internal organization of the project, importance of the human resources of the project, importance of its budget, average unit cost per course, per participant, etc.

Qualitative evaluation of results V

1 Objectives

This type of evaluation concerns the progress, efficacy and value of courses and permits feedback action on programme evolution at any time. Provision may in fact be made for the measurement of results so as to ensure the weekly[1] supply of selected information to the regional level concerning progress. This will enable the regional director (or supervisor) to be informed immediately of any obstruction to the evolution of the programme as planned, to investigate the causes of delay or interruption and to take steps affecting the programme itself, or the instructor, so as to improve the situation. The instruments available on the spot will also make it possible to improve both the educational material employed and the professional capacities of the instructors. Finally, evaluation makes it possible to measure at any given moment the level of knowledge acquired by participants in the course of their literacy and vocational training.

2 Scope

This type of evaluation will furnish information concerning:
The participants' success at end-of-cycle tests. The 'end-of-cycle report' (see Appendix, Document 3) lists, for each test, the number of items, the critical threshold, the average score obtained, the number of participants tested and the number and percentage of successes.

[1]. Or fortnightly, or monthly, according to circumstances.

The level attained by participants each week,[1] throughout the duration of the programme. The 'monthly report' (see Appendix, Document 2) indicates, at 'G', the results of weekly tests, and for each test the number of participants tested, the critical threshold and the percentage of successes. If the project provides for weekly pre- and post-testing, each column at 'G' in this monthly report may be subdivided into two parts and thus provide additional information, with particular regard to the previous level of knowledge of the participants (certain superfluous items of information might well be omitted) and to their capacity of immediate retention.

The above data, which should be collected systematically, may well be supplemented by more comprehensive information concerning the tests, so as to permit analysis of the results in greater depth. In this case, a procedure of sampling may be adopted in place of automatic inclusive recording, on the basis of two types of report:

A summary of all the marks obtained by the participants of the sample groups in end-of-cycle or end-of-programme tests, which will permit the calculation of statistics of averages, of dispersion, or of totals.

The percentages of success obtained for each item, either in periodical (weekly or monthly) or in end-of-cycle tests, which will permit item-by-item analysis and detailed determination of the knowledge acquired by participants.

3 Instruments

In addition to the instruments for systematic data collection and for sampling mentioned above, the devices most frequently used will be tests.

Definition of testing

The International Psychotechnical Association defines 'testing' as a specific trial involving the performance of a task, identical for all the subjects examined, coupled with a precise technique for the appreciation of success or failure or for the numerical notation of success. A valid test, the construction of which is a lengthy and complicated process, should possess the following characteristics among others:

1. Or fortnight, or month, according to circumstances.

Effectiveness: it should actually measure what it is intended to measure. For greater assurance its results should be compared with an external criterion.

Reliability: it should permit continuous measurement of a given phenomenon. This requires homogeneity or internal consistency, stability in time and objectivity.

Sensitivity: it should be capable of distinguishing qualitative or quantitative changes in a scale of units adapted to the phenomenon under investigation.

It will be worth while, at least as far as tests of occupational knowledge are concerned, to make certain that they do indeed possess the above qualities and that they are consequently to a certain extent predictive. But since the investigations involved—because of their complexity—will not normally be undertaken in the context of literacy projects, we should more properly speak of 'standardized trials' rather than 'tests'.

The rigorous measurement of results depends on three categories of tests which should be prepared with the greatest care. These are: initial tests, which determine for each participant the 'take-off' point of his/her knowledge; terminal tests, which indicate the level of knowledge at the end of the cycle or the programme; and interim tests, which should if possible be applied weekly.

Literacy scale

The acquisition of knowledge can only be measured if the initial level of knowledge is known beforehand. This implies pre-testing, preferably by means of the 'literacy scale' (see Appendix, Document 5) adapted from the test devised by C. Maguerez.[1] This scale permits the classification, in an ascending order, of basic skills in reading, writing, counting and calculation. On the basis of the results obtained at the outset of the cycle (literacy scale) and at the end of the cycle (terminal tests which will be described below), individuals are classed at three levels:

Level I. Classification is given to illiterates, i.e. to individuals who can neither read, write or count, or who—at best—can decipher a few letters or perform a few very simple calculations. It should be noted that this definition, which corresponds to grades 0, 1 and 2 on the literacy scale, is not the counterpart of that which Unesco applies to a 'literate', i.e. one capable of drafting a brief account of his daily activities;

Level II. Classification is given to semi-literates, i.e. to individuals

---

[1]. C. Maguerez, *La Promotion Tehnique du Travailleur Analphabète*, 1966. (In French only.)

who should be capable of deciphering written or printed phrases (without necessarily understanding their sense) and possibly of writing (or rather, copying) a text, but who are incapable of utilizing these aptitudes for cultural or socio-economic purposes. Complex numerical sums are generally beyond them. They are frequently persons who once started to learn, but who have since abandoned their studies or forgotten what they learned for want of constant practice. This level corresponds to grades 3 and 4 on the literacy scale;

Level III. Classification is given to individuals whose knowledge and aptitudes correspond to four or five years of primary schooling, and who may be considered to be 'literate' according to the Unesco definition. This level corresponds to grades 5 and 6 on the literacy scale.

The literacy scale tests are applied to each participant at the time of registration. Comparison of these results with the results of end-of-cycle tests will make it possible to determine whether the individual concerned may be declared literate.

End-of-cycle tests

These tests should include as a minimum:[1]

A test of reading, writing and spelling, designed to measure the degree of comprehension of a written or printed message and proficiency in spelling. Use should be made wherever possible of actual documents that the participant is called upon to handle, such as administrative forms to be completed, publicity material describing agricultural products about which the participant can be questioned, etc.

A test of arithmetic designed to measure the participant's grasp of number and basic operations; this may be accompanied—if the initial level of knowledge of the participant so permits or if the technicality of the programme so requires—by tests involving the calculation of fractions, percentages, scales, time-spans, etc.

A test of arithmetic applied to a professional problem and designed to measure the participant's ability to apply the knowledge acquired to the mathematical solution of practical issues affecting his occupation or daily existence.

A test of the capacity for self-expression in writing, including the use of symbolic language; for example, drafting a letter explain-

---

1. The EWLP project in Iran constructed a number of quality tests which might well serve as examples.

ing why it has been decided to adopt a new technique recommended by the programme, illustrated by a sketch, drawing or explanatory diagram.

If possible, a practical test of know-how, designed to show that the participant is capable of applying technical/vocational skills acquired during the course.

One or more tests, according to the content of the programme, in the technical subject taught (rice-planting in rows, cotton-growing, weaving and spinning, child care, co-operative farming, etc.).

One or more tests in general culture: history, geography, religion, civics, politics, etc.

The form taken by these tests will obviously depend on educational practice in the country concerned, but efforts should be made to ensure the greatest possible degree of standardization. It should be borne in mind that the application of standard tests to all groups of participants in the same programme will permit inter-group comparison, and is thus preferable to the application to each group of separate tests constructed by the instructors concerned. Moreover, the construction of standard tests at project headquarters, by persons having more time and opportunity than the instructors to shape them according to the principles set out above, will enhance their validity and reliability. Needless to say, the components of the tests should reflect the objectives of the programme teaching, and should consequently be based on what is actually taught (i.e. credibility of content). Finally, standard tests permit easy and objective marking, since the most frequent types of answer will have been foreseen and the manner of marking determined with precision. Further, the form of the questions, which will generally be of the multiple choice or true/false type, implies short answers which lend themselves to rapid correction.

Periodical tests

Periodical tests covering the essentials of what is taught and the difficulties encountered during a given period may be constructed for each sequence or group of sequences. These tests, which may be global or subdivided into as many items as there are programme components, may be applied at the beginning and/or end of the sequence/group of sequences. Note can be taken of the percentage of correct answers to each question.

4 Descriptive studies

The documents described above will provide lists of results which may be broken down test by test, item by item, group by group and individual by individual; they will permit the preparation of a series of descriptive tables of results according to the region, instructional technology or sponsoring body concerned. For example:

2-1 [1] Results of initial tests (by region, instructional technology, sponsoring body).
2-2 Results of end-of-cycle (first or second) tests of elementary arithmetic (Indicator 7a).
2-3 Results of tests of applied arithmetic (Indicator 7b).
2-4 Results of tests of the ability to read with comprehension (Indicator 7c).
2-5 Results of tests of the ability to express a simple message in writing (Indicator 7d).
2-6 Results of tests written from dictation.
2-7 Results of tests of occupational/technical knowledge (Indicator 8).
2-8 Results of tests of socio-economic knowledge (Indicator 9).
2-9 Results of tests of knowledge of health, hygiene and nutrition (Indicator 10).
2-10 Results, in percentages of success, of the item-by-item analysis of all the relevant tests undertaken.
2-11 Results of all (or of the most important) weekly tests, including average scores and percentages of participants passing the critical threshold.

5 Comparative studies

Some of the tables mentioned above are periodical, and thus permit comparisons not only within and between groups but also diachronically. This involves:
The classification of literacy centres according to the results of different tests and the identification of those where performance was significantly above or below average. For this purpose it will be necessary to calculate the average scores obtained in each test, the percentage of successful participants (or the overall average if the groups concerned are all of more or less the same size), variants within and between groups, etc. It may then be possible to detect the causes of conspicuous failures or spectacular successes merely by correlating the figures obtained with other internal or external variables, such as the personal characteristics of the instructors, environmental, logistic or climatic factors, etc.

1. The numbering is carried on from that used in Chapter IV, Section 3.

The analysis of item-by-item results, which will permit the instructor — provided that a record is kept of the percentages of success in each item of each weekly test — to identify the weak points of his teaching. At the regional level, analysis of these results from all the groups will point to weaknesses in programme content, since the identification in the majority of the groups concerned of the same failure with regard to a given item (or group of items) may well indicate that the corresponding element of the curriculum has been ill-conceived, and perhaps that the curriculum may have been drawn up too hurriedly.

The analysis of individual results permits *inter alia* the control of individual progress. This analysis may be carried out at the local level (for the benefit of the instructor), at the regional level, or at project headquarters by means of random sampling. Analysis of results by groups of participants will also make it possible to distinguish between 'good' and 'less satisfactory' instructors. Correlation of these results with the personal characteristics of the instructors concerned may help in drawing a portrait of the 'ideal' instructor.

These comparative studies, if they cover both end-of-cycle and weekly (or fortnightly or monthly) tests, should therefore make it possible to follow the progress of teaching in each course and in each group of courses with great accuracy. Consequently, as soon as a course or group of courses is seen to be yielding unsatisfactory results, the supervisor is alerted, and it becomes feasible to identify the weakness rapidly and to take action with regard to the instructor, the environment, the teaching process or the content of the course itself. Such feedback action should produce effective results and permit considerable savings in expenditure. Finally, comparative studies may help in the task of defining the features of the ideal instructor, or the optimum size of a group, or the logistical, environmental or other factors on which its success depends.

6 Explanatory studies

If the project has the necessary means, further studies may be undertaken with the aim of identifying the causes of success.

Some hypotheses

At this stage, attempts may be made to verify a great number of hypotheses by applying classical statistical procedures to the correlation on the one hand of the results of different tests, and on the other of different variables which may be internal or external as far as the literacy action is concerned, but which should preferably be selected in the upstream sections of the functional literacy process (for a conceptual diagram of this process, see Chapter IX, Figure 6). It is no more possible here than in the preceding chapter or in those that follow to draw up an exhaustive list of possible hypotheses for verification, since these will depend on the projects themselves. Nor is it recommended that attempts be made to verify all the hypotheses set out below, or all those which the EWLP team attempted to verify as set out in the Appendix (Document 8).

Hypotheses concerning political will

Do participants achieve better results when there exists a political will to provide literacy training with a view to transforming the milieu?

A correlation may be plotted between a 'results of tests' variable and a variable constructed from data provided by the feasibility study (cf. Chapter III, Section 3 (i)). Political will might be assessed by means of a composite indicator covering, for example:
The number of visits by prominent politicians and senior officials.
The number of interventions by non-governmental organizations, trade unions, women's groups, scout movements, churches, etc.
Interventions by local literacy committees.
Etc.
If statistical calculations suggest that the answer to the question above is in the affirmative, the authorities might be invited to support projects more effectively if and when new literacy centres are established.

Hypotheses concerning the autonomy of the project

It may be asked whether better results depend on a higher degree of autonomy of the project (in terms of the region concerned, the instructional technology involved or the sponsoring body responsible) (cf. Chapter III, Section 3 (ii)), or on the greater rationality of its organization. On this theme the average results obtained by each group in the different tests may be correlated with indices which measure the degree of autonomy or rationality of the project, with the help of a composite indicator which might cover:
The degree of local or regional integration of the project with a development operation.
The degree of integration of the project with the local or regional authorities representing the sponsoring ministry.

The degree of local or regional autonomy of the bodies responsible for the execution of the project.

The degree of autonomy of the project with regard to other bodies responsible for adult education.

Etc.

Verification of the hypotheses concerning project autonomy—and of those concerning political will—can have little direct bearing on the project concerned, since it is difficult to modify the situation profitably while the programme is under way. But the studies involved are of considerable theoretical interest, since their results will make it possible to improve the preparation of new projects.

Hypotheses concerning financial resources

It may justifiably be asked whether better results depend on increased financial resources for the group (or region or instructional technology). Here, the results obtained in tests may be correlated with the expenditure on each group. The construction of the 'financing' variable presents no difficulties; we shall return to this indicator in greater detail in the next chapter.

Hypotheses concerning human resources

The question here mainly concerns instructors, and the field of investigation is broader and more easily accessible. Verification of various hypotheses will, quite obviously, be for the most part carried out within the projects, since study of the inevitable correlations between the results obtained in tests and the main characteristics of the instructors and of their training should permit identification of the features which distinguish an instructor who obtains the best results from a given population and programme. On the basis of these studies, action will be taken to recruit as future instructors only those who passess such characteristics, and to provide them with the training which appears likely to produce the best results.

Hypotheses concerning the possibilities of the environment

An attempt can be made to verify certain hypotheses concerning the environment by correlating the average scores obtained in tests with certain indicators which measure the facilities which the environment offers (cf. Chapter III, Section 5 (iv) and (vi)), such as:

Voluntary participation by pupils in the construction of a classroom for literacy courses.

The existence of a local literacy committee; support from leading personalities.
The existence of an organized village structure.
The existence of communication facilities.
The existence of a public health infrastructure.
The existence of an educational infrastructure.
The existence of a supporting infrastructure for agricultural development.
Etc.

Use will be made here either of a composite indicator or of a twin-series coefficient of correlation. Verification of these hypotheses is of use in determining the minimal environmental conditions required for a new project to have reasonable chances of success.

Hypotheses concerning the characteristics of participants

Success in tests may without difficulty be correlated with the characteristics of participants, and this correlation will permit better identification of those who are most successful: women or men, young people or adults, land-owners or agricultural labourers, etc. Scores obtained in all (or certain) tests may also be correlated with participants' previous levels of academic knowledge or vocational skills, with their degree of familiarity with the language of instruction, with their level of success during the preceding cycle, with the extent to which they are active in local affairs, in the organization of courses, etc.

Familiarity with the conclusions of this type of investigation will permit project leaders to improve the constitution of groups; for example, by according preference in the recruitment of participants to persons possessing characteristics which correspond to those of the most successful students in the preceding group, by according more attention to participants with unfavourable characteristics in order to bring them up to the level of the others, or by investigating the causes of failure in these less-favoured categories with a view to taking remedial action.

The results obtained in these tests may also be correlated with certain indicators noted during the preliminary studies concerning participants and related to their motivations, interests, etc. (cf. Chapter III, Section 3 (v)). This should make it possible to assess the degree of predictability of the motivation surveys (validity testing), and thus to determine whether certain failures were foreseeable while the project was still being prepared. The following elements could be investigated:

The expressed desire to learn, above all to read, write, calculate, etc. (comparison should be made with results obtained in the corresponding tests).
Other forms of learning desired (in connection with professional, family or social life).
Benefits obtained from literacy (increased income, new occupation, social prestige, improvement of daily living conditions, etc.).
Assessment of the difficulty of different learning processes.
Assessment of potential obstructions to the will to learn.
Etc.
It is obviously possible, if the project has the means of doing so, to carry the analysis still further by calculating the correlations with reference to different characteristics of the participants: age, sex, marital status, number of children, salary or socio-economic status, etc.

Hypotheses concerning educational methodology

The hypotheses for verification here are those concerning educational means and methods which are listed as 8 to 14 in the Appendix (Document 8), and which will be considered in greater detail in Chapter VII.

Hypotheses concerning the tests themselves

Studies concerning the tests themselves are designed chiefly to verify their effectiveness: sensitivity, validity and forecasting efficiency, reliability, homogeneity and objectivity (cf. Section 3 above); and to improve them. The procedure to be followed involves the internal examination of each test, followed by a series of inter-test studies with the aim of verifying that the sequences employed truly correspond to the planned objectives. The greater part of this task should have been completed before the application of the tests, but—as we have already pointed out—the conditions under which projects are executed do not generally permit this.

Studies of this type call for access to the results of tests carried out on a certain number of groups belonging to a selected sample, to the results of tests carried out on a sample of participants, and to the item-by-item results of a certain number of other tests. The identity and dimensions of the samples will be determined with due reference to the studies envisaged. All these data, collected with the aid of the instruments described above (and cf. Appendix, Documents 2 and 3), should make it possible *inter alia:*

To investigate the diagram of the results of each test, to verify the normality of its curve and spread (sensitivity of the test).

To study the homogeneity of each test: inter-correlation between items, inter-item consistency, etc.

To compare the results of certain tests with an external factor. For example, the level of attainment in a functional literacy programme involving reading, writing, arithmetic, etc., may be evaluated by comparing this attainment with that of pupils in a given class of a regular school. In order to make this comparison, it will be necessary to apply to the functional literacy participants (or to the school pupils) the relevant tests for both programmes, and then to correlate the results of each series of tests (apparent validity). One may also compare the results of a weekly test of vocational skills or know-how, for example, with an on-the-spot assessment, by a foreman, of the participants' actual workshop performance at the end of the programme (predictability factor).

To study the inter-correlations of tests, and thus to determine *inter alia* whether the tests are self-contained or, in fact, contain certain elements in common. Study of the inter-correlations between tests of the first cycle and final tests of the second cycle should make it possible to determine which of the former have the highest predictability factor with regard to success in the second cycle.

To investigate multiple correlation coefficients, which should furnish better knowledge of the degree of predictability of the association of the different tests employed, and permit the establishment, if so desired, of weighting coefficients for each.

To carry out a factorial analysis which may make it possible to isolate the principal factors of this type of learning process. It can only be hoped that this factorial analysis will reveal a structure in which 'technical apprenticeship' is predominant, closely followed by 'reading', 'arithmetic' and 'numeracy'.

Etc.

Evaluation of the impact of the logistic components of the project

VI

1 Objectives

Chapters IV and V dealt with ways and means of evaluating the quantitative and qualitative results of literacy action: presentation and description of these results; comparisons between them and with the criteria of success; and investigation of the probable causes of the situations which gave rise to those results. Chapter V was limited to the possible influence on results of variables related to the characteristics of participants and instructors (actors and intermediaries, respectively, in the process of literacy training), and of variables related to the environment in which training is conducted: political will, infrastructure, human resources, etc.

The study of these factors, which are all more or less external to literacy action *per se*, has not been included in the present chapter, since it appears preferable to distinguish between those areas in which the project team has no authority (selection of the population or zone to be rendered literate, environment, political will), and those where the project team is free to act as it sees fit, to exercise its authority and responsibility and to experiment, modify, eliminate or invent.

Chapter VII will also cover areas in which the project team is sovereign, but which are internal to the literacy action: the methods, content and materials of teaching. Here, therefore, we shall be more particularly concerned with logistical matters: organization, management, planning—in which the executive team of the project is fully master of the action.

2 Scope

Here the task is to investigate the extent to which the quantitative and qualitative results of courses are affected by such logistical elements as:

(i) The choice of the locality—not the area—and premises where courses are to be held; time-table; number and duration of sessions; duration of the programme.

(ii) The principal characteristics of the groups: homogeneity by sex, age, socio-economic status, occupation and qualifications; stability, effect of additional registrations; participants/instructor and instructors/group ratios; functional adequacy of the programme.

(iii) The material organization of the groups: basic equipment; supply of teaching materials (quantity and nature); supervision; type of transportation; aid in kind (foodstuffs, etc.).

(iv) The internal organization of the project: qualifications of research and executive staff; qualifications of instructors and supervisors; links with development bodies; visits to centres by project directors.

(v) Volume of investment and recurrent expenditure.

3 Instruments

The information required for the investigation of the subjects listed above will come from two sources, within and outside the project.

Internal information

This will come for the most part from the 'course sheet' (see Appendix, Document 6) drawn up by the instructor, possibly with assistance from the supervisor, one month after the course has begun, and transmitted to the regional office of the project. Part A of this document will furnish data concerning 2(i) above; Parts B and C cover 2(ii); Parts F and G will cover most of what is required by 2(iii); Parts B and E cover 2(iv); and Parts H and J will provide some of the information required under 2(v) for purposes of partial verification.

The 'monthly report' (see Appendix, Document 2) provides at 'B' information concerning supervision; at 'C' information concerning teaching material; at 'D' information concerning assistance (e.g. food) received; and at 'E' partial information concerning the budget.

All the data furnished by these documents may be combined

Information concerning the budget

The task here is not to carry out a cost/benefit analysis, but to attempt to determine a few unit costs, knowledge of which will be essential for the planning of expenditure if at any moment an extension of the literacy action already in progress is envisaged. Although it will as a general rule be preferable to entrust this task to the financial specialists of the ministry sponsoring the project, an outline plan for the evaluation of unit costs is set out below.

This evaluation will call for vital information from two sources: the budget, and extra-budgetary resources.

Budgetary expenditure should be subdivided into:

Staff costs for (a) headquarters (management, services; if possible, research personnel should be listed separately); (b) supervisors and general service staff at the regional level; (c) instructors; (d) fellowships (indicate the functions of the fellowship-holders, as above).

Equipment costs (distinguish between project headquarters and regional and local levels): (a) buildings; (b) furniture; (c) vehicles; (d) teaching material. If possible, list equipment costs for research separately.

Maintenance costs (distinguish between project headquarters and regional and local levels): (a) water, electricity, heating; (b) building maintenance and repairs; (c) vehicle maintenance and repairs; (d) consumables (chalk, classroom cleaning materials, etc.); (e) food; (f) travel expenses (supervisors); (g) training-courses, etc., for personnel; (h) miscellaneous costs. If possible, list maintenance costs related to research separately.

Income. List separately income derived from:

The national budget.

Local or regional authorities (grants, personnel, vehicles, free water and electricity, aid in the form of food, etc.).

International organizations.

Bilateral aid.

Development bodies (para-public or private) to which projects may be attached.

Non-governmental organizations (political parties; trade unions; churches; women's and youth organizations, etc.); individual donations.

4 Descriptive studies

The data furnished by the means described above will permit the establishment of a list of indicators which may initially be presented in descriptive tables. Provision will have been made in advance for the adequate classification of the data collected, with their variants and scales. A simple consultation of the descriptive tables will provide the various teams with a picture of the material state of each course and of its evolution. The tables, which should be drawn up separately for each region, instructional technology and sponsoring ministry, will include gross totals, percentages and a certain number of statistics of averages and dispersion, as set out below (the numbering follows that adopted in the earlier chapters):

3-1 Distribution of courses by location: open-air; specially assigned premises; schools; workshops; community halls; church premises, etc.

3-2 Distribution of courses according to the distances to be covered by participants.

3-3 Distribution of courses by timing: morning; during the midday break; evening; after the evening meal; before or after shifts, etc.

3-4 Distribution of courses by average length of session and number of sessions per week.

3-5 Distribution of courses by duration of the programme and placing in the calendar year.

3-6 Time-table of the project (by region and instructional technology) with indications of meteorological conditions (rainfall), time-table and impact of agricultural activities and number of sessions planned for each separate month.

3-7 Distribution of courses by sex (women, men, mixed) and age group (below 15, 15-25, 26-45, above 45) of the groups of participants.

3-8 Distribution of courses by professional occupation and level of qualification of participants.

3-9 Distribution of courses by number of additional registrations.

3-10 Distribution of courses by participants/instructor ratio.

3-11 Distribution of courses by instructors/group ratio.

3-12 Distribution of courses by quantity and nature of teaching material received (collective, individual, or for instruction).

3-13 Distribution of courses by amount of basic equipment provided (the calculation will depend on individual projects).

3-14 Distribution of courses by method of transportation employed by participants.

Evaluation of the impact of the logistic components of the project

3-15 Distribution of courses by quantity of aid in kind received (food, clothing, accommodation, etc.).
3-16 Distribution of courses by technical aid related to professional occupation (paid leave of absence or permission to attend courses during working hours, gifts of fertilizers or pesticides, product of harvest on demonstration plots, etc.).
3-17 Distribution of courses by number and type of supervisory visits.
3-18 Distribution of supervisors by number of courses under their responsibility.
3-19 Distribution of instructors (and supervisors) by sex and age group;
3-20 Distribution of instructors and supervisors by professional origin (schoolteachers or members of the teaching profession, peasants, workers, rural extension workers or other officials, foremen, specialists, etc.) and by professional qualification (unskilled, skilled, specialist, technician, etc.).
3-21 Distribution of instructors and supervisors by seniority in their regular professions and experience in literacy teaching.
3-22 Distribution of management and research staff by category (civil servants, local officials, workers under contract for the project, development agency officials; foreign specialists, etc.), and by professional grade (senior officials, middle-level officials, general service staff, etc.).
3-23 Distribution of courses according to the degree of organic relationship with socio-economic development operations (e.g. the percentage of sequences directly linked with the occupational content of the programme).
3-24 Distribution of courses according to instructor's status, i.e. employee of the socio-economic development agency or employee (full-time, on detachment or under contract) of the literacy project.
3-25 Distribution of income by calendar year according to source (State budget, international organizations, bilateral aid, local communities, development bodies, non-governmental organizations, miscellaneous) and designation: staff costs, equipment, miscellaneous.
3-26 Distribution of staff costs according to region, instructional technology and sponsoring body, as assigned to: managerial and headquarters staff; supervisors and general services; instructors; fellowships.

3-27 Equipment costs for buildings, furniture, vehicles, teaching material: at project headquarters and at local and regional levels.
3-28 Maintenance costs according to item (see Section 3 above): at project headquarters and at local and regional levels.
3-29 Research costs by category (staff, equipment, operational); annual figures.
3-30 Average unit costs, according to sponsoring body, region and instructional technology, per group of participants; supervisor; instructor; registered participant; participant dropping out during the first cycle; participant dropping out during the second cycle; participant successfully completing the first cycle; participant successfully completing the second cycle.

The figures for the majority of these tables should be calculated by calendar year.

5 Explanatory studies

No attempt is made in this chapter to provide examples of the comparative studies between groups or periods which can be carried out on the basis of the broad range of indicators listed above. But a comparison of the annual figures resulting from such studies may indicate that certain regions or instructional technologies are receiving more support than others, and thus permit project directors to adjust their strategies accordingly.

We shall be more concerned here with studies of the explanatory type and with the following hypotheses, which may be tested with the help of the abundant data described above.

Hypotheses concerning the organization of courses

It may be asked whether factors connected with the organization of courses have a bearing on the figures which reflect the quantitative and qualitative results of literacy action. The answer will be found by correlating data from Tables 3-1 to 3-5 above with data from monthly and end-of-cycle reports (see Chapter IV and Appendix, Documents 2 and 3), which may be built up into tables similar to those described in Chapter IV, Section 3, Tables 1-5 to 1-15, concerning drop-outs. This correlation will permit affirmative or negative replies to the following questions.

Do the rates of coverage, turnover, drop-outs, attendance, time utilization, participation in final tests and success in end-of-cycle tests vary with the type of premises selected for the courses?

Do these rates vary according to the distances (beyond a given minimum) which participants must cover to attend courses?
Are these rates affected by the time of day chosen for the courses?
Are these rates significantly affected by the duration of daily sessions, the weekly number of sessions or the length of the cycle?
Are these rates affected by the time of year at which courses are held?
Experience has shown that further analysis is required in many cases. It will, for example, be worth while, with regard to hypotheses such as those concerning the distance travelled by participants or the time of day selected for the courses, to investigate the behaviour of the participants according to sex and age.

Hypotheses concerning the constitution of groups

Similar studies may be undertaken with the aim of determining the extent to which the composition of groups (homogeneous or otherwise) affects the indicators listed above. Data from Tables 3-7 to 3-11 should be correlated with data from tables providing various rates in respect of basic indicators of participation in programmes and of acquired skills (Chapter II, Section 4).

This correlation will reveal the influence of group homogeneity (by sex, age, socio-economic status, occupation, qualifications, level of previous education, language) and indicate the types of homogeneity to be sought during the constitution of different groups in order to obtain the best results.

Hypotheses concerning the material aid provided

The same procedure can be adopted for the correlation of data from Tables 3-12 to 3-18 with data related to the basic statistical indicators. This will make it possible to determine whether the different rates which measure the results of courses are modified by variations in:
The amount of basic equipment.
The amount of teaching material provided for the course.
The distance covered by participants and the type of transport involved.
The amount of assistance in kind (principally foodstuffs).
The amount of other forms of assistance.
The degree of supervision.

Hypotheses concerning the financing of courses

It will be interesting to test certain hypotheses relative to the influence of the volume of expenditure on the results obtained. Such investigations can be conducted at various levels, e.g. according to region, to instructional technology, or to combinations of the two. Studies may be carried out down to group level, provided it is possible to identify expenditure on equipment and maintenance, and provided the average unit cost per instructor or supervisor for the region, or for the instructional technology concerned, is known.

For each aggregate retained, calculations will be made of the costs of equipment (buildings, educational materials, furniture), of overheads and of consumables, and the figures obtained will be correlated with the different rates described above.

Similar calculations and correlations may be made with regard to average unit costs of groups and participants. This may make it possible to determine whether the volume of expenditure indeed affects success and, if so, which items of expenditure are of the greatest importance.

If average unit costs for certain groups (both as a whole and per participant) are ascertained, these figures may usefully be correlated with figures concerning success in tests, absenteeism, etc. This could reveal a pattern of interrelationships which cannot but interest those responsible for the financing and the strategy of the project.

Evaluation of programme content VII

1 Objectives

The aim here is to verify that the programmes taught actually correspond to the planned objectives of the teaching; that they are indeed the most economical in financial and pedagogical terms; and therefore the least costly, the most easily taught and the most rapidly assimilated.

This is primarily a matter of determining whether the programmes are suited to the assigned social and economic objectives, to the sociological and psychological characteristics of the population concerned and to the fundamental principles of the literacy method selected: in short, of determining whether the method employed is a true functional literacy method.

Secondly, the question is one of costs and benefits. The aim is to discover the best programme for leading the maximum number of participants to final success in the shortest time.

2 Scope

There are two approaches to this evaluation. The first involves verifying whether the programmes actually lead in the direction of the assigned objectives. In other words, we ask the question: Is what is intended to be taught actually taught, in the manner intended and, consequently, is what is intended to be measured actually measured? In this connection, it should be recalled that the ultimate object of measurement is the cultural, social and economic impact of literacy action on the population concerned. We shall deal with this issue in Chapter VIII.

The second approach involves the quest for the most adequate programmes, i.e. those which are most economical, not only in financial terms but also—and doubtless above all—in terms of the effort demanded of participants during the process of learning.

Criteria exist for the first of these approaches. They comprise: the list of planned objectives; the problems which have been identified and which the proposed teaching must endeavour to solve; and the interests and expectations of the individuals concerned. All these criteria will have been determined during the preliminary studies.

For the second approach there exist criteria which may *à la rigueur* be adopted, in the shape of the classical or traditional standards adopted in each country for the measurement of school attainments (reading, writing, arithmetic, etc.). But literacy projects are not intended for children: they are intended for individuals for whom —whether they are adults or adolescents—the classroom (which is in any case an artificial universe, remote from day-to-day realities) represents an alien world. There are no standards or yardsticks of attainment for the programmes offered to such individuals. Instead, the programmes themselves must be specifically designed and special criteria of success devised in each case. In the universalist type of education such as that provided in schools the criteria of success have been laid down by usage; in an education based on problem-solving such as functional literacy training these criteria depend on the problems themselves. Thus virtually every case will call for innovation, and innovation implies experimentation before generalization.

Hence the evaluation of the content of literacy programmes covers two ranges of inquiry: the verification of the degree of adequacy of the programmes in terms of the planned objectives, which will be considered in sections (i) to (iii) below; and the organization of pedagogical experimentation (sections (iv) to (vi)). It will obviously be impossible here to deal with all the issues involved, and we may well ask whether all the problems have been considered, let alone solved, in other types of education (school, university, re-training and in-service training of adults, education of the physically or mentally handicapped, etc.). We must limit ourselves to indicating the main fields which might be covered by research and to suggesting some of the directions which might be taken by such research, if the projects have the means and opportunity to make it feasible.

(i) *Adequacy of programme with regard to objectives*

In the early pages of Unesco's *Practical Guide to Functional Literacy*, published in 1973, C. Bellahsène stresses that the effectiveness of functional literacy training depends to a very great extent on its matching up to the objectives and problems of the development of the socio-economic milieu in which it is to be conducted; and that prior definition of an operational strategy which takes account of this basic requirement thus constitutes the crucial stage in any intervention.

In follows that before the impact of this intervention is measured, the evaluator must ascertain that such a matching up to objectives and problems actually exists at programme level, by verifying that the different aims of the training inherent in each literacy programme coincide:

With the economic and/or social objectives defined during the preliminary studies and explicitly listed in an order of priority by the responsible authorities (cf. Chapter III, Section 2).

With the technical/vocational and social-economic objectives defined by the technicians and selected for priority attention from the outset as intermediate goals on the path to the broader social and economic objectives determined by the political authorities (cf. Chapter III, Section 4).

With the problems listed during the preliminary studies concerning the achievement of the technical/vocational and socio-economic objectives in terms of capacities, aptitudes and behaviours at work and in human relations, together with reactions to the geographical, economic, social and cultural environment (cf. Chapter III, Section 4).

With cultural and educational objectives in the case of literacy projects not directly related to social or economic development. Here the question is merely one of drawing up an inventory of academic knowledge.

(ii) *Adequacy of programmes with regard to the population concerned*

Adequacy in this respect is considered to be a fundamental principle of the functional literacy method. Its verification involves the necessity of determining whether the planned programme takes account of the results of the motivation survey and the investigation of the milieu (Chapter III, Section 3 (v) and (vi)), and more specifically whether it respects: the planned selection criteria: geographical or cultural area, age and sex, occupational or social category; certain specific characteristics of the population with regard to professional category and qualification and language; certain manifest interests and motivations of the participants (i.e. whether the programme corresponds to individual expectations).

(iii) *Concurrence of the evolution of the programme with the original plan*

Here it is necessary to verify: whether the sequences have developed in the order and on the dates originally planned; whether all the planned components have in fact been taught; whether the planned order of progression has been respected.

These studies will be undertaken with the aim of identifying the psychological causes of certain failures in the programme's adequacy in terms of the intellectual capacities of the participants, but not the causes of failure in the operation of the project as a result, for example, of its organization or environment.

(iv) *Adoption of basic methodological principles*

The task here is to evaluate, by use of experimental groups (see Chapter II, Section 4, C), the importance in terms of the costs and benefits of the project of certain basic pedagogic principles peculiar to functional literacy, e.g.:
The integration of theoretical and practical training.
The integration of literacy teaching with other elements of instruction at the level of sequences and sessions.
The principle of inclusiveness: this involves listing all the components of each instructional technique: reading, writing, drawing; numbers, calculation, elementary arithmetic, applied arithmetic, geometry, etc.; personal hygiene, professional hygiene, nutrition, health, prevention of illness, accidents, etc.; history, geography; all the vocational techniques taught, etc.
The principle of diversification of technologies, techniques and instruments: this involves listing the specific pedagogical characteristics of each instructional technology: sequences, components, order in which sequences are taught, instruments (books, posters, cassettes, radio and television broadcasts, instructors' manuals, technical guides, etc.). For each instructional technique the number of units (sequences, books, components, etc.)

common to each programme, the number common to several programmes, and the number of units which are absolutely unique to a single technique should also be noted.

The principle of adaptation of material to the educational method employed, to the professional characteristics of the instructor and to the intellectual characteristics of the participants.

(v) *Special educational methods*

Experimental groups may also be used for an investigation of the most profitable methods to be applied to each programme component. Since the nature of such experiments will, as a general rule, depend on specific situations, and frequently on the degree of importance attached by the methodologists to different aspects of the educational problems as they arise during the course of the programme, we shall mention only a few of the possibilities:

Learning to read: global or analytical methods.
Learning to write: with or without prior training in graphics.
Learning arithmetic: 'functional' or traditional progression; speed in studying numbers, the reading and writing of numerals as a separate exercise or at the same time as words, etc.

(vi) *Teaching materials employed*

This subject is also very broad, since it covers not only the traditional scholastic materials which project leaders will be tempted to employ because they have proved their worth or because of a conformist attitude, but also materials which are specific to each instructional technology or specific to adult education (in post-literacy teaching, for example), and so-called 'modern' materials, notably audio-visual.

These materials may be grouped in the following categories:

Materials designed for individual use by participants

For reading: primers, grades I and II, technical kits, mobile letter boards, reading cards, special booklets (tales, proverbs, poems), technical brochures, etc.

For writing: exercise books, cards, etc.

For arithmetic: textbooks of elementary and applied arithmetic, notebooks, cards, etc.

Miscellaneous: drawing-books, diaries, etc.

Materials designed for collective use
Problem-posters, sets of mini-posters, photographs, drawings, figurines or 'flanellographs'.
Self-correcting kits for reading, arithmetic, technical subjects, etc.
Phonetic tables (for reading), multiplication tables, geographical maps, various synoptic tables (health, technology).
Mobile letter panels.
Calendars, etc.

Audio-visual materials
Material for collective use (as above).
Wall or other newspapers.
Mural materials.
Films for cinema or television.
Slides and film-strips.
Radio and television broadcasts.
Tape-recordings, etc.

Materials for instructors' use:
Specialized manuals for reading, writing, arithmetic, etc.
Operating manuals for audio-visual or other technical equipment.
Information sheets and guides for occupational teaching (livestock-raising, cotton-growing, spinning, weaving, child nutrition, accident prevention, etc.).
Cassettes, films, slides, radio educational programmes, etc.
Material for teachers' information and cultural improvement (correspondence courses, etc.).

3 Instruments

Here, as in the previous chapter, evaluation is multifaceted and its instruments are extremely varied. Efforts should be made in all cases to select those techniques which are the most objective and which lend themselves to easy statistical processing. But subjective processes such as experts' judgements must also be employed.

(i) *Experts' judgements*

The evaluator will turn to expert judgement only in cases where observation and appreciation cannot be related to measurable criteria.

The process involves inviting a large number of specialists to judge a particular situation and to express their conclusions on a scale of the type:

5, perfect; 4, very satisfactory, 3, satisfactory; 2, relatively satisfactory; 1, unsatisfactory.

or

5, very high standard; 4, high standard, 3, acceptable (many favourable elements), 2, not adequate; 1, totally inadequate or virtually useless.

The marks given will then be averaged.

Expert judgement of this kind will be used primarily for determining:

Whether programmes are adequate in terms of the general objectives (cf. Section 2 (i) above). In this specific case the task may be entrusted to members of the *ad hoc* committee set up during the organization of the project (cf. Chapter III, Section 2 (vii)).

Whether programmes are adequate with regard to the criteria of selectivity and specificity of the population for which they are intended. The experts will classify programmes according to a five-point scale:

5, highly selective/specific; 4, adequately selective/specific; 3, moderately selective/specific; 2, barely selective/specific; 1, in no way selective/specific.

In the cases just mentioned, recourse to the subjective opinion of specialists on the issue under consideration is preferable to the utilization of pseudo-objective instruments such as percentages of ambitions or motivations expressed, which pose problems of weighting coefficients and of measurement of sincerity.

(ii) Monthly report

The monthly report (see Appendix, Document 2) indicates at 'F', for each component of the programme, the number of sessions planned and actually held during the month and the number of taught and untaught sequences. It also indicates at 'G' the results of weekly tests.

(iii) End-of-cycle report

This report (see Appendix, Document 3) provides the results of final examinations in each subject.

(iv) Course sheet

The course sheet (see Appendix, Document 6) provides all the relevant information concerning the teaching material available and used in each course.

(v) *Tests*

Tests have been dealt with in Chapter V, Section 3 above, and questionnaires and interviews in Chapter II, Section 2.

(vi) *Experiments*

These should be planned in great detail by a team comprising a methodologist, specialists in syllabus construction, an educational psychologist, an expert in the principal technological subject taught, an administrator for material and financial questions and a specialist in evaluation. This team will determine the content of the experiment, the number of groups involved, the instruments to be employed (type, content, etc.), the duration of the experiment, the manner in which the data will be processed and presented, the cost of the operation, etc.

4 Descriptive studies

These studies will be based on the tables built up from data collected by the instruments described above. The most important of these tables will include:

4-1 Distribution (monthly, quarterly or by cycle) of courses according to the number of sequences delayed or untaught in each area and in each instructional technology.

4-2 Distribution (monthly, quarterly or by cycle) of courses according to the number of sequences (or sessions) taught in each programme component, by area and by instructional technology.

4-3 Malfunctioning of courses: distribution of courses by region and by instructional technology according to the category of reasons given by instructors for any malfunctioning: external reasons (unsuitable premises, excessive distances to be travelled by participants, lack of materials, unfavourable meteorological conditions, etc.); internal reasons (excessively demanding programme, excessive speed, absence of interest, lack of utility, etc.); personal (fatigue, illness, incompetence, maternity, overwork).

4-4 Distribution of courses as above, 4-3, according to reasons for malfunctioning given by participants.

4-5 Distribution of teaching material designed for individual use, according to instructional technology and type of material, by categories.

4-6 Distribution of material designed for collective use, according to instructional technology and type of material, by categories.

Evaluation of programme content

4-7 Distribution of audio-visual material, according to instructional technology and type of material, by categories.

4-8 Distribution of material designed for instructors' use, according to instructional technology and type of material, by categories.

4-9 Degree of selectivity of programmes according to geographical or cultural area, occupation, social category, etc., of participants: by type of selectivity retained, by instructional technology and by expert assessment (marks 5 to 1).

4-10 Degree of specificity of programmes according to professional activities (branch, sector, product), qualifications, language, etc.; by instructional technology, type of specificity retained and expert assessment (marks 5 to 1).

4-11 Degree of adequacy of programmes with regard to the main interests and motivations expressed by the population concerned: by instructional technology, type of interest or motivation retained and expert assessment (marks 5 to 1).

4-12 Distribution of instructional technologies according to percentage of programme time reserved for practical training (monthly figures if necessary).

4-13 Distribution of instructional technologies according to degree of integration (marks 5 to 1) at the level of the sequence and at the level of the session.

4-14 Distribution of instructional technologies according to the number of sessions devoted to each programme component: reading, writing, arithmetic, technical training, health, drawing, history, civic instruction, etc.

4-15 Distribution of instructional technologies according to specific or common pedagogical characteristics: sequences, components, teaching instruments, etc. (see above, Section 2 (iv)).

4-16 Expert judgements: table of assessments of the adequacy of programme contents with respect to each of the economic objectives retained, by objective, instructional technology and marks accorded (5 to 1).

4-17 Expert judgements: table of assessments of the adequacy of programme contents with respect to each of the technical/occupational or socio-economic objectives retained, by objective, instructional technology and marks accorded (5 to 1).

4-18 Expert judgements: table of assessments of the adequacy of programme contents with respect to problems concerning capacities (intellectual and vocational knowledge to be acquired), skills (know-how), behaviour (professional respect for standards of safety and hygiene), attitudes to modernism, participation, development, etc.), environment (struggle against harsh conditions, natural disasters, epidemics, etc.); by instructional technology, by problem retained and by marks accorded (5 to 1).

4-19 Expert judgements: table of assessments of the adequacy of programme contents with regard to pedagogical objectives (knowledge and skills to be acquired) and to psychological objectives (development of the capacity to memorize, analyse and synthesize, of attention, judgement, transposition, etc.); by instructional technology, objective retained and marks accorded 5 to 1).

5 Explanatory studies

In the field of evaluation of literacy programmes and as far as instructional technologies are concerned, the scope for experimentation is virtually limitless. We shall therefore confine ourselves here to one or two hypotheses for possible verification under each of the headings above. It will be noticed that the majority of the studies mentioned below contain, at some point or other, a comparative element; this is why 'comparative studies' as such are not shown separately in the present chapter.

(i) *Hypotheses concerning the adequacy of programmes with regard to the objectives of the project*

In the preceding chapter the question arose whether an improvement in the logistics of a project might lead to an improvement in its quantitative and qualitative results. We shall now ask whether maximum adequacy of programmes in terms of project objectives might have the same effect.

The following procedure could be adopted for the construction of an index of adequacy, the economic objectives having been listed in order of priority during the preliminary studies for the project. Application of the technique of expert judgement will have made it possible to attribute to each programme (or instructional technology) a figure which is the average of the marks attributed by the experts in respect of its adequacy in terms of each of the objectives (Table 4-16 above). This series of averages is correlated in turn with each series corresponding to the various ratios calculated (Chapter III, Section 4) for each instructional technology, i.e. with the indicators concerning turnover (ratios of registration, attendance, participation in tests, etc.)

and with the indicators concerning success (Chapters IV and V). The different correlations will make it possible to determine whether there is a relationship between the two types of data, and to measure the importance of the correlation coefficient so calculated.

(ii) *Hypotheses concerning the adequacy of programmes with regard to the populations concerned*

In the same manner, we may construct indices of measurement of this type of adequacy. With the instructional technology in question as a point of reference, data from Tables 4-9, 4-10 and 4-11 will be used to construct an index representing the average of the marks attributed by the experts to each component of these tables. The marks thus attributed to each instructional technology will then be correlated with the different ratios obtained with regard to participation, drop-outs, absenteeism, success in tests, etc. The correlation coefficients so calculated will suggest a number of conclusions, and these in turn will make it possible to determine whether a high degree of adequacy of programmes with respect to the populations concerned, in terms of selectivity, specificity and regard for their own interests, has a favourable influence on the quantitative and qualitative yields of the courses taught.

(iii) *Hypotheses concerning the progress of the programme*

It may be asked whether the causes of malfunction in a programme lie in failures in the organization of the courses, or within the structure of the programme itself. In the first case the answer may be found by correlating data from Tables 4-1 to 4-4 above with data from Tables 3-1 to 3-30 in Chapter VI. The data selected for comparison, of course, should reflect any strong *a priori* indications concerning those causes. Thus, for example, it will be worthwhile investigating whether certain decisions with regard to the choice of premises and timetables, certain characteristics of the group (sex, age, qualifications), certain aspects of material organization (assistance received), certain characteristics of the instructors (sex, age, socio-professional homogeneity) or finally certain features of expenditure (equipment, maintenance, average cost of the group) have a statistically significant influence—either positive or negative—on the progress of courses.

Data from Tables 4-1 and 4-2 may be correlated with data from Tables 4-3 and 4-4, which indicate the different reasons given by instructors and participants for the malfunctioning of courses.

Lastly the data contained in Tables 4-1 to 4-4 will provide indispensable evidence for use in verifying hypotheses formulated during the process of experimentation. Some of these hypotheses are set out below.

(iv) *Hypotheses concerning the basic pedagogical principles of the functional literacy method*

Points (i)—(iii) above dealth with hypotheses the verification of which makes it possible to determine firstly whether programmes planned for the project respect the basic strategic principles of functional literacy action (adequacy with regard to economic objectives and to the population concerned; selectivity; specificity) and, secondly, whether respect for these principles actually enhances the results of the action. The task now is to determine, with the aid of the following hypotheses, whether the basic pedagogical principles of functional literacy are respected in the programmes and—when this is so—whether the quantitative and qualitative results of those programmes are correspondingly better.

It should be pointed out that although affirmative answers to the above questions will indicate almost beyond doubt that, for the adults of the country concerned, the functional method offers the best form of literacy training, it will still be necessary to demonstrate that its direct economic, social and cultural impact on the population is both real and significant. The ways and means of providing this demonstration will be considered in the next chapter.

Hypotheses concerning different forms of integration. Integration is a fundamental pedagogical principle of functional literacy training. We have seen above how it is possible to assess the degree of integration of programmes with objectives and with the milieu. We shall now examine ways and means of evaluating the effects of pedagogical integration.

This process involves verification of the following hypotheses:

The results of functional literacy training, measured by the ratios of attendance, success in tests and normal functioning of the programme (cf. (iii) above), are better when practical demonstration or—better still—the practical application of know-how is integrated with theoretical teaching than when practice and theory are kept apart.

The results measured as above are better when different components are integrated (e.g. reading and mathematics with technology and drawing, etc.) than when each component is taught separately.

The results are even better when different subjects (reading, writing,

arithmetic, drawing, technology) are incorporated in the same lesson than when they are treated separately.
Verification of these hypotheses involves the construction of matched group samples and the application to each set of groups of a curriculum which is different in terms of form, time-table, teaching materials and instructional guides, but identical with all the others in terms of objectives, content and the number and order of sequences and sessions. This experiment should start at the beginning of the cycle and continue over a relatively long period of time. The data collected will be incorporated in Tables 4-12 and 4-13.

Hypotheses concerning the principle of inclusiveness. The functional literacy method implies all-round training of the individual. The hypothesis may be advanced that the broader the scope of the programme of teaching, the greater the participation and the higher the success in final tests. To verify this hypothesis, data from Table 4-14 will be correlated with the different ratios of attendance, success and normal functioning of the programme. The investigation may be pursued further by breaking down different components into subcomponents, e.g. mathematics into numbering, reckoning, elementary arithmetic, applied arithmetic, geometry, conversions, scales, etc.; or health into personal and occupational hygiene, illness and accident prevention, nutrition, child nutrition, pre-natal hygiene for expectant mothers, etc.

Hypotheses concerning the diversification of techniques and instruments. As an inevitable corollary of the problem-solving approach, without which there can be no functional literacy, diversification—whether of instructional technologies, components, content, presentation, priorities, or instruments (books, posters, cards or sheets, cassettes, radio, television, etc.)—is an obvious feature of functional literacy programmes. Table 4-15 will yield an index which can be correlated with the different ratios of attendance, success in tests and normal functioning of the programme.

Additional hypotheses for verification under this heading might concern the adaptation of pedagogical material, the type of method employed, the characteristics of instructors and the level of previous knowledge (intellectual and technical) of participants.

(v) *Hypotheses concerning special pedagogical methods*

Attention will be centred here on reading, writing and arithmetic. Similar interim tests in these subjects will be applied to groups of participants matched in terms of behaviour and results, and percentages of success will be calculated for each item. Efforts will be made to eliminate the effects of extraneous variables such as organization, environment, etc. The final (or intermediate) results from these experimental groups will be correlated with relevant data for the same groups bearing on such items as costs, duration of the learning process, participants' opinions concerning difficulties, quality of retention, etc., and of course with basic criteria such as the various ratios of attendance, success in end-of-cycle tests and smooth functioning of the programme.

The purpose of this experimentation is to identify and perfect the teaching methods which are best suited to the population groups concerned, for each of the main programme components. The field here is virtually unlimited, and it will be advisable to refer to specialized treatises on adult education. A few examples of subjects to be considered are set out below:

For reading: global, analytical, mixed, etc., methods; learning to read without learning to write; high or low degree of integration of the process of learning to read with other programme components, etc.

For writing: choice of script; learning to write with or without previous graphic training or practice in manual dexterity; high or low degree of integration with other mainly technical programme components (function).

For mathematics: integration or non-integration with other (principally technical) subjects; speed in acquiring numeracy; previous learning not based on the decimal system but traditional in the group concerned; 'academic' or 'functional' syllabuses, etc.

For the new vocabulary (generally technical): learning with or without reading and writing.

For programmes taught in a language other than the mother-tongue: relative speeds of learning the new language, orally or with reading and writing, etc.

Etc.

(vi) *Hypotheses concerning the material employed*

It may be asked, with regard to each type of material employed, whether its content matches the initial objectives, whether it is logically constructed, whether it is psychologically suited to the level of the participants, whether it corresponds adequately to their interests and is consequently capable of holding their attention, whether the language employed is easily understood, whether the illustrations are well adapted, etc.

Numerous hypotheses may also be advanced with regard to technical aspects of the production of this material: in the case of books, for example, their cost, durability (in terms of both form and content), layout, etc. General questions of this nature may also be accompanied by more specific investigations, such as:

Books: most suitable type size; space between letters, words and lines.

Posters: typographical research as in the case of books; investigation of most suitable methods of illustration (offset, photography, line drawings, etc.); assurance that the images and symbols employed pose no problems of comprehension.

Cassettes: investigation of problems related to comprehension of the language used, speed of delivery of spoken texts, silent pauses; problems of handling, maintenance, etc.

Radio, television: research as in the case of cassettes; investigation of problems related to listening or viewing times, length of broadcasts, retention, etc.

Evaluation of predicted changes VIII

1 Objectives and general methodology

The central hypothesis of functional literacy declares that literate individuals become more effective agents in the process of socio-economic development. This implies that functional literacy training should have a marked and favourable impact on the way of life of the individuals concerned and on the economic development of the region in which they live.

The relevant changes should be measured on both a medium- and a long-term basis, since literacy action may, under certain circumstances, have an initially negative and subsequently positive influence on the economy. In the case of a programme designed to improve coffee production, for example, if the effect of a course of functional literacy has been to convince planters that they should renew their stock by radical pruning every five years, the result will be a marked reduction in output during the first two years after pruning and a probably significant increase during the third and fourth years, while maximum production will only be reached after the sixth year.

Similarly in the case of individuals, the measurement of change must be approached with caution. Innovation in a stable society may have far-reaching ramifications, especially when the innovation is of an intellectual nature. The volume and the speed of transfer are related positively to the degree of abstraction in the teaching provided; and the depth of change in the pupil's outlook becomes considerable.

The investigation of change, which should be carried out at both the individual and the collective levels, comprises an initial stage during which expected changes, already built into the objectives of the programme, are identified, delimited and then measured at each level; and a second stage during which the changes so measured are compared, both in nature and extent, with those originally anticipated.

The method employed will be that of diachronic comparison of matched samples (control and experimental), as described in Chapter II, Section 4. Verification of the selected hypotheses will therefore require statistical instrumentation capable of indicating:

Whether positive changes in terms of economic and social development are occurring in villages where a literacy centre has been established (experimental sample A).

Whether positive changes are occurring in villages where there is no literacy action (control sample B).

Whether the changes in area A are indeed due to literacy and not to other forms of action, such as agricultural extension work.

Whether literacy action carried out in conjunction with other forms of action is more effective than when it is conducted in isolation.

Whether the changes attributed to literacy action occur harmoniously or whether they have a disturbing effect on the society concerned.

Etc.

2 Scope

Here the scope for evaluation of the external type is very large, since it includes all those quantifiable aspects of human activity which may be modified as a result of subjecting the individuals concerned to literacy training. The practical limits of the evaluation will therefore be determined by the limits of the objectives once these have been precisely stated; and both the criteria of change and the indicators and indices of measurement employed will be those which are best suited to ensure valid results. We use the term 'criteria of change' to cover all those areas, or parts of areas, which are susceptible to modification under the anticipated impact of the literacy project. By 'indicators' we mean those variables or phenomena the presence and measurement of which are essential to any appreciation of the effectiveness of the project; such indicators should be practical and should lend themselves to easy measurement and manipulation. The unit of measurement should be chosen in such a way as to permit an easy differenciation of values. We shall frequently be concerned with several variables which it will be more logical and practical to group together in order to extract a single value (or 'index') which will be considered as an indicator.

The Appendix to this guide contains a list of 'Dimensions, Criteria and Indicators' for a programme of functional literacy training (Document 7) comprising tables which might serve in the quest for indicators which will normally have been identified before the construction of a questionnaire (cf. Chapter II, Section 2).

This same Document 7 sets out the major fields of human activity in which it is hoped that functional literacy training will stimulate favourable change. These fields are recapitulated below, while Technical Document VI of the 'Global Evaluation of EWLP' series *(Alphabétisation Fonctionnelle et Développement: Les Effets Economiques et Sociaux du Processus d'Enseignement-Apprentissage)* provides a comprehensive description of the type of research that might be carried out in this connection, as for example:

The will to change.

The ability to learn.

The will and the ability to integrate with the social and cultural environment; ability to plan, to organize and to solve problems (prospective dimension); ability to obtain and communicate information (cognitive/acquisitive and heuristic dimension); ability and will to co-operate (integrational dimension).

Desire to control the material and human milieu: ability, know-how and action for production; ability, know-how and action to sustain the capacities for living and working productively.

The will to transform the economic and psycho-cultural environment: improvement of living standards (economic dimension); acceptance of change and innovation (attitudinal dimension).

It should be pointed out that the domains, criteria and indicators contained in this table are provided as examples only; the list is neither a minimum nor exhaustive.

3 Instruments

The evaluation of the economic and social impact of functional literacy training will involve use of most of the instruments described up to now, but more particularly questionnaires, observation sheets and interviews. Only two remarks are called for here:

(i) *Tests of ability*

In many cases, it will be necessary to differenciate between the 'know-how' acquired by the participant during literacy training and the 'action' which confirms his will to change and to adopt new techniques, reflecting his favourable attitude to innovation. Document 4 in the Appendix to this guide provides an example of a test of know-how. Tests of this kind should be constructed by the evaluator in collaboration with the project methodologists and the agricultural technician or engineer in charge of the undertaking.

(ii) *Construction of indices*

The technical field in which a diligent evaluator can search for possible indicators is practically limitless; but at the data-processing stage, the correlation of an abundance of mini-indicators with other variables may demand such a vast amount of work that the evaluator may well be obliged to abandon a number of otherwise useful indicators. In such cases, the problem may often be solved by constructing indices (i.e. aggregates of indicators) against which the criticism will sometimes be levelled that they are arbitrary or even false. This poses problems related to representativity and coefficients, and the evaluator will have to turn to techniques which belong to the field of tests and examinations.

Some examples of the construction of indices are set out below:

Index: 'Improved Methods of Rice Growing'. One point is awarded for affirmative answers to each of the following questions:

  Is the farmer taking steps (on a minor scale) to modify or improve, i.e. to control, the water supply?

  Is he using fertilizers?

  Is he cultivating recommended high-yield varieties?

  Is he applying improved methods of cultivation officially recommended for his area (e.g. re-planting in rows)?

  Is he wherever possible replacing the traditional method of treading the soil with oxen (as in Madagascar, for example) with mechanical methods?

  Is he double-cropping wherever possible?

  Is he taking steps to protect his crops against insects, rats, birds?

Index: 'Anti-erosion Measures'. One point is awarded for affirmative answers to each of the following questions, which should be posed at the level of the community:

In forest zones, is the practice of cultivating on burnt-out ground decreasing?
Is the amount of wood-cutting on hilly ground or on fragile soils decreasing?
Are there fewer bush-fires (which destroy the vegetable cover)?
Is cattle-breedig controlled so as to discourage local erosion by over-grazing?
Is reafforestation in progress?
Is terraced farming practised on hilly ground, and do the terraces follow the contour lines?

Index: 'Importance of Changes Aimed at Improvement in Matters of Hygiene, Health and Nutrition'. Points are awarded as indicated, and their total constitutes the index:

During the year, the person concerned:

Has suffered from attacks of malaria	− 1 point
Has suffered from bilharziasis	− 1 point
Has suffered from intestinal infections	− 1 point
Has been treated preventively or curatively for bilharziasis	+ 1 point
Has been treated preventively or curatively for malaria (quinine treatments)	+ 1 point
Has been vaccinated (or had his children vaccinated)	+ 1 point
Consults a doctor or nurse in case of illness	+ 1 point
Washes every day	+ 1 point
Makes regular use of soap	+ 1 point
Washes his clothes once a week	+ 1 point
Uses a toilet	+ 1 point
Takes garbage to a proper dump	+ 1 point
Looks after hen-runs, stables, etc.	+ 1 point

The above list may be lengthened with questions concerning purity of water, nutrition, childcare, etc.

4 Descriptive studies

A large number of descriptive studies of situations at different stages of the literacy action may be made on the basis of data drawn from tables of indicators concerning predicted economic, social and cultural changes.

It is essential to gather initial data before the action is launched, since this will permit intermediate investigations designed to determine whether the socio-economic status is indeed beginning to evolve, and to apply feedback action to programme content (mid-course correction) if it appears that the situation is not developing as initially planned.

Similar surveys will then be conducted at regular intervals after the initial programme of literacy training has been completed, since certain anticipated changes may occur only slowly, and it is rare to observe attitudinal changes which provoke rapid modifications of social or economic behaviour. Time must be allowed for the interplay of different phenomena: reflection, maturation, rejection of alien concepts by the corporate body, together with positive echoes and stimuli from new generations of literates (the more new literates appear on the scene, the more rapidly the planned changes will occur).

The areas in which these changes should occur are very broad and cannot all be dealt with in tables here. But the Appendix contains a list of dimensions, criteria and indicators of change designed for a programme of functional literacy training for a group of mine workers many of whom cultivate a plot of land. This list may serve as an example for other projects.

5 Comparative studies

The external evaluation of the socio-economic impact of functional literacy action is an exercise which lends itself readily to comparative studies. Indeed, comparisons could at a stretch be made with virtually every indicator.

In investigations of a pedagogical nature, the following procedure will be adopted: variants in form or content of a single element of the teaching process (e.g. use of a particular manual, application of a given method, experimentation with a given sequential or integrated system, etc.) are applied to different groups which have been carefully matched to ensure the greatest possible similarity as far as other vaiables are concerned.

The performances of these groups are compared before the experiment begins (by testing the hypothesis of homogeneity of variance, for example) to confirm that they are indeed similar. The results of this test will be A for the experimental group, and a similar, or statistically insignificantly dissimilar, B for the control group. At a second stage, and after the experiment, a similar comparison of new performances (A' for the experimental group, B' for the control group) will be made by means of the same homogeneity test, to determine whether—in accordance with the initial hypothesis—there is now a significant difference between the new results. If this is the case, the initial hypothesis is confirmed.

Results A and A' are then compared, as are results B and B'. The differences between the former should be greater and more statistically significant than the differences between the latter; and the difference (D) due to the literacy action, as measured by the experiment, can be expressed:

$$D = (A' - A) - (B' - B)$$

The above example concerns comparisons made within the literacy action. Other comparisons may be envisaged between groups of participants receiving literacy training and groups receiving other forms of adult education, e.g. farmers following an agricultural extension course or industrial workers following a course of in-service training. Here, after these courses, a comparison may be made of technical performance or the application of recommended innovations as between the participants in these literacy training programmes and control groups of still illiterate farmers or workers. Participants in functional literacy training programmes may also be compared with participants in traditional programmes.

In order to avoid dispersal and duplication, studies related to external evaluation are all dealt with together in Section 6.

6 Explanatory studies

As in the preceding chapters, we shall mention a number of studies which may be undertaken to test simple hypotheses formulated on the basis of the list of assigned objectives.

Data for these studies will for the most part be provided by tables constructed from the indicators described in Document 7 of the Appendix (cf. Section 2 above). Certain of the hypotheses involved were tested by the team responsible for the global evaluation of EWLP, which formulated them differently (see Appendix, Document 8).

In the final chapter of the guide we shall return to the subject of global evaluation of a literacy project, which has already been touched upon in the foregoing chapters.

(i) *Hypotheses concerning the will to change*

Hypotheses in this category will be verified by reference to the earlier motivation surveys conducted during preliminary research on feasibility of the project (see Chapter III, Section 3 (v)). The basic hypothesis will be that the adults whom the project has just made literate were, before the project began, more outspoken than those who have remained illiterate in expressing the will to change and in adducing more weights and varied motivations for their desire to acquire:

The basic techniques of literacy (reading, writing, arithmetic).

Knowledge concerning the means of production (origins of the firm employing them, importance, expansion, activities of other employees, etc.).

Knowledge concerning openings available in the profession (technical training, in-service training, promotion).

Intellectual knowledge required in the exercise of their profession (calculation of weights, volumes, dynamics, speeds, outputs, etc.; design and draughtsmanship, etc.).

Knowledge related to the specific technology of their job or occupation.

Knowledge concerning the conservation and enhancement of their productive energies.

Knowledge related to their physical and geographical environment (physical geography, astronomy, meteorology, etc.).

Knowledge related to economics (money, trade, costs, taxes, etc.).

Knowledge regarding the social, political and religious world (history, civics, trade-unionism, workings of society and the State, etc.).

A further hypothesis may be advanced, namely that, before the project began, the participants, in comparison with non-participants:

Provided a greater number of motives for wishing to become literate.

Estimated more accurately the time which would be required to become literate.

Expressed a keener desire to change their occupations or jobs.

Expressed a keener desire to travel, emigrate, change their horizons.

As it was impossible at the time of the preliminary surveys to construct experimental and control samples, the same questionnaire will be submitted to participants in the first days after registration and a matched control group will then be constructed.

(ii) *Hypotheses concerning integration with the social and cultural milieu (prospective dimension)*

The hypothesis may be advanced that literate adults are more likely than illiterates to adopt a form of behaviour that implies better planning for the future. This prospective dimension will be examined under three headings: 'Schooling of Children'; 'Economic Planning'; and 'Family Planning'. Data will be provided by the indicators described in the Appendix, Document 7.

Schooling of children: The task here is to determine whether the children of literate adults are put in school to a greater degree than those of illiterates, and whether drop-outs are less frequent among the former than among the latter. This investigation may be carried out by means of diachronic comparison of matched samples of participants and non-participants in literacy courses. Overall scholarization and drop-out ratios for villages where literacy courses are being held may also be compared with the same ratios as applied to the children of participants in the courses.

Economic planning: The analysis of household budgets is dealt with in (vii) below. Here we are concerned with verification of the following hypotheses:
Literate individuals attempt to increase their incomes.
Literates more frequently keep household accounts.
Compared with illiterates, literate consumers spend less on food, more on health, hygiene, leisure, etc.
Literates are more inclined to adopt modern methods of investment.
In borrowing (and lending), literates prefer modern methods (banks, credit unions, etc.) to traditional methods (usury).
Literates store up more reserves and stocks and organize these reserves in line with advice provided during their training.
Literates invest more than illiterates in productive or essential goods, and less in non-productive goods or items for display.
Literates tend to acquire durable goods as recommended during their training.
The indicators retained for verification of the above hypotheses should be related directly or indirectly (intellectual transfer) to the teaching received, including recommended innovations.

Family planning: Four hypotheses for verification might be that, in comparison with illiterate adults, literates:
Have fewer children.

Leave greater intervals between the births of their children.
Make greater use of contraceptive methods.
Desire fewer children.

(iii) *Hypotheses concerning insertion into the social and cultural milieu: cognitive/acquisitive and heuristic dimension*

The hypothesis may be advanced that adults who have received functional literacy training more willingly adopt forms of behaviour leading to self-determination in the quest for knowledge, without need of direct outside stimulation. Verification of this hypothesis involves testing the following three sets of propositions:

Use of the mass media: Literates resort more freely to the mass media, more frequently and for greater lengths of time; they make greater use of the mass media for their individual economic, social and cultural advancement (selective listening or viewing, search for technical information in the press, etc.).

Social and informative use of reading and writing: New literates tend to make greater use of correspondence for obtaining and imparting information; they make greater use of public administrative facilities through forms and circulars; they create their own personal 'data banks' in the form of diaries, notebooks, almanacs, etc.

Use of other sources of information and aid: Literate adults formulate more requests for advice, opinions or technical assistance from professional or welfare organizations, banks, family counsellors, etc., and travel more widely and frequently in search of information or with the aim of improving their patterns or standards of living.

(iv) *Hypotheses concerning insertion into the social and cultural milieu: integrational dimension*

The hypothesis may be advanced that adults who have received literacy training are keener to participate more fully (and presumably to co-operate more effectively) in the different collective organizations of their communities, and thus favour the development of solidarity and concertation. A number of subordinate hypotheses may be envisaged on the basis of indicators identified and retained during research along similar avenues.

(v) *Hypotheses concerning control of the material and human milieu (with regard to production)*

The hypothesis may be advanced that the technical ability of the

Evaluation of predicted changes

literate adult, in all productive activities, is higher than that of the illiterate, and that the same is true in the case of behaviour at work because the literate adult is more familiar with working habits which are likely to enhance production.

Data from the tables contained in Document 7 in the Appendix to this guide may be used to verify the following hypotheses:

In comparison with illiterate adults, adults who have undergone literacy training:

Improve their professional qualifications during the course of this training.

Receive more favourable reports from their superiors on the shop floor (engineers, technicians, foremen) concerning the quantity and quality of their work.

Are less prone to absenteeism and more inclined to punctuality.

Show greater respect for safety regulations and have fewer, less serious, and less incapacitating accidents.

Show, in their attitudes to machinery and tools, a greater degree of knowledge and comprehension of technical-productive practices (respect for norms, more regular maintenance, cleanliness of machinery and its surroundings, adoption of innovations or improvements in agricultural practices, etc.).

Are increasingly less wasteful of materials and time.

Are more inclined to request, and more assiduous in attending, in-service training courses (spend more time on such courses, more frequently and at a higher level of training).

Are less inclined, when the same incentives are offered to illiterates (in-service training, agricultural extension courses), to resist the adoption of modern technical and productive practices designed to increase output.

Are more inclined to adopt, and more ambitious in the adoption of, rational technical and productive standards (agricultural timetables, methods of cultivation, processes of craftsmanship, etc.).

Are quicker to adopt, on a larger scale, modern or new products (fertilizers, selected seeds, new crops, etc.).

Etc.

(vi) *Hypotheses concerning control of the material and human milieu (with regard to the conservation and restoration of productive energies)*

The hypothesis may be advanced that literate adults more willingly adopt modern practices with regard to the conservation, restoration and reproduction of vital and productive energies, and that among literates, as compared with illiterate communities:

Vaccination and other prophylactic methods of combatting epidemics are in greater use.

Recourse to modern medicine in case of illness or childbirth is more frequent.

Infant morbidity and mortality rates are decreasing.

More households keep stocks of medicine.

More time is spent on personal hygiene (baths, showers, dental care, etc.).

The diet is more varied.

There is greater respect for food hygiene (use of filters, boiling milk, water, etc.).

(vii) *Hypotheses concerning the transformation of the economic milieu*

We come, finally, to hypotheses the verification of which will permit the evaluator to determine whether the literacy action undertaken has achieved its ultimate objective, which is the transformation for the better of the economic and psycho-cultural milieu. The first task is to verify whether living standards have improved, by comparing data on incomes, collected from samples of participants and non-participants both before and—at regular intervals—after the literacy project. These comparisons will make it possible to confirm or invalidate a certain number of hypotheses according to which, in literate as opposed to illiterate communities:

Monetary income is higher.

More members of one family are wage-earners.

The average net global monetary income, per member of the family, is higher.

The factors of production are more varied.

The volume of debt is in decline.

The means of production are superior in quantity, nature and value (equipment related to production, maintenance, transport).

The volume of production is higher.

The value of production is higher.

The patrimony is greater.

The consumption of durable goods is higher.

Expenditure on life-style (improvement of housing, consumption of non-productive goods) is higher.
Homes are more comfortable.
Etc.

(viii) *Hypotheses concerning the transformation of the psycho-cultural milieu*

The final hypotheses presume that newly literate adults, as compared with illiterates:

Have more ambitious projects for their children's future.
Have more positive ideas concerning women and their place in society, marriage, questions of dowry.
Are more anxious to participate in social development.
Are more willing to accept modern solutions to problems raised by development.
Have a deeper desire to continue to learn.
Are more inclined to accept scientific explanations of natural phenomena.

Global evaluation of the project IX

The chapters above have shown how studies may be conducted in each of the main fields covered by evaluation.

If the necessary resources are available, the more ambitious task of global evaluation of the project may be attempted, on the basis of explanatory theoretical models of each of the main fields examined.

1. Quantitative evaluation of results

Instead of merely verifying the hypotheses set out in Chapter IV, the evaluator may attempt to construct an explanatory theoretical model, as illustrated in Figure 2; its verification will permit identification of the conditions under which optimum attendance (i.e. minimum drop-out and absenteeism) is obtained. This will require calculation of the correlations between the different factors proposed.

This model is based on the potential influence of six independent factors (left and centre of the diagram) and one semi-dependent factor (top-right—success in interim tests) on the dependent factor of attendance. Investigation of these correlations might make it possible to determine the group characteristics most likely to ensure optimum attendance at courses.

The evaluation of literacy programmes

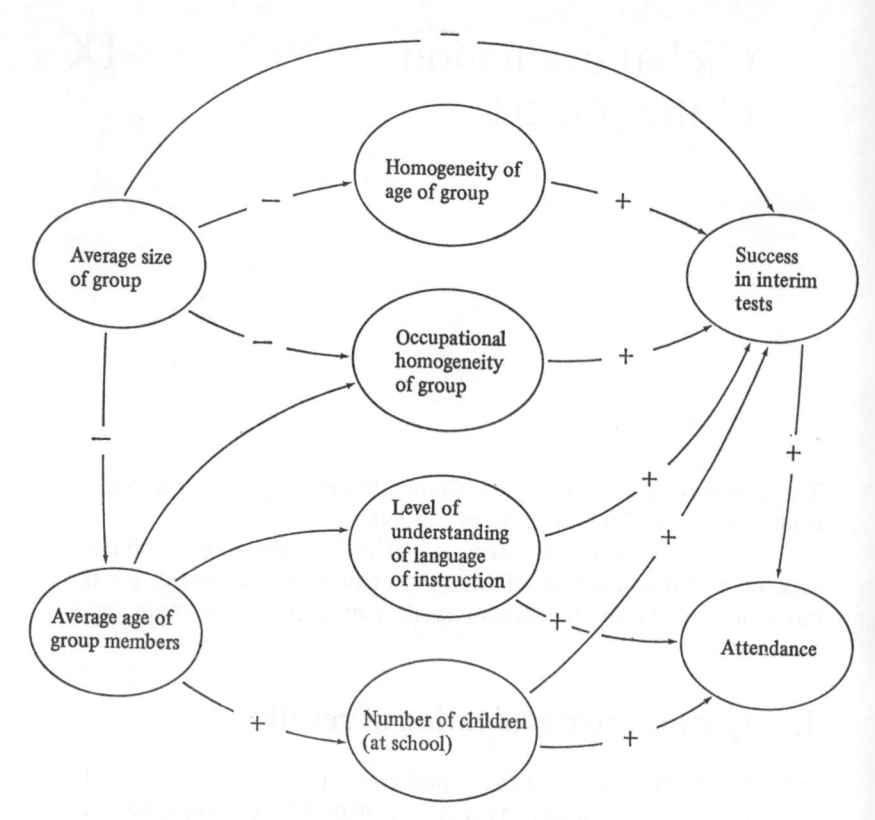

FIG. 2. Explanatory theoretical model for optimum attendance.

2 Qualitative evaluation of results

The evaluator may go beyond the mere verification of hypotheses, numerous examples of which were provided in Chapter V, and attempt to construct different explanatory theoretical models bearing on success in tests.

The final technical report of the Iranian pilot project in functional literacy for adults contains a large number of examples, on which the model set out below (Fig. 3) has been based. Three sets of factors are incorporated here: participants; groups of participants; and instructors.

It is assumed that homogeneity within the group (with regard to age, socio-economic status, professional activity, professional qualifications, level of previous education and possibly sex) has a positive influence on results in tests. It is also assumed that identity or similarity of levels with regard to age, professional activity, socio-economic status and possibly sex concerning the instructor and the participants also has a positive influence on these results. In Figure 3, the different factors are linked by positive or negative signs, corresponding to positive or negative influences either presumed or actually verified, totally or in part, in the Iranian pilot project. The factors contained in boxes in the diagram (group stability and specificity/adequation of the programme) may be connected with theoretical models from Chapter IV (optimum attendance), Chapter VI (optimum functioning of the project) and Chapter VII (optimum specificity and adequacy of the programme from the standpoint of participants).

The organization of the process of data analysis may be left to the specialists, although it would appear that Wroclaw's method of taxonomic analysis—despite its disappointing results during the evaluation of EWLP, due to the inadequacy or lack of reliable data—should give satisfactory results, provided that the project can provide data from a large number of programmes. If such data are available, it will be possible to construct an optimalized model which may serve for the elaboration of new programmes. To do this, it will be essential to obtain all available data from all the literacy programmes constituting the project (see the indicators described in Chapters VI, VII and VIII), to define the criteria of success in tests and to construct an 'index of success'. An effort will then be made to classify the programmes by type according to the degree of success obtained and using the established criteria. Then, in order to refine the analysis still further, the evaluator will attempt to identify, in each programme, the principal elements contributing to its success, and to attribute values to these elements. Finally, on the basis of this double appreciation, which is both descriptive (by virtue of the order, classification and values attributed to the different variables) and explanatory (by virtue of the study of interactions and the verification of hypotheses), it will be possible to propose an optimum model programme for the population concerned, with due regard to its geographical, economic, cultural and social environment and to the content of the teaching proposed.

This type of many-faceted analysis should make it possible to determine:

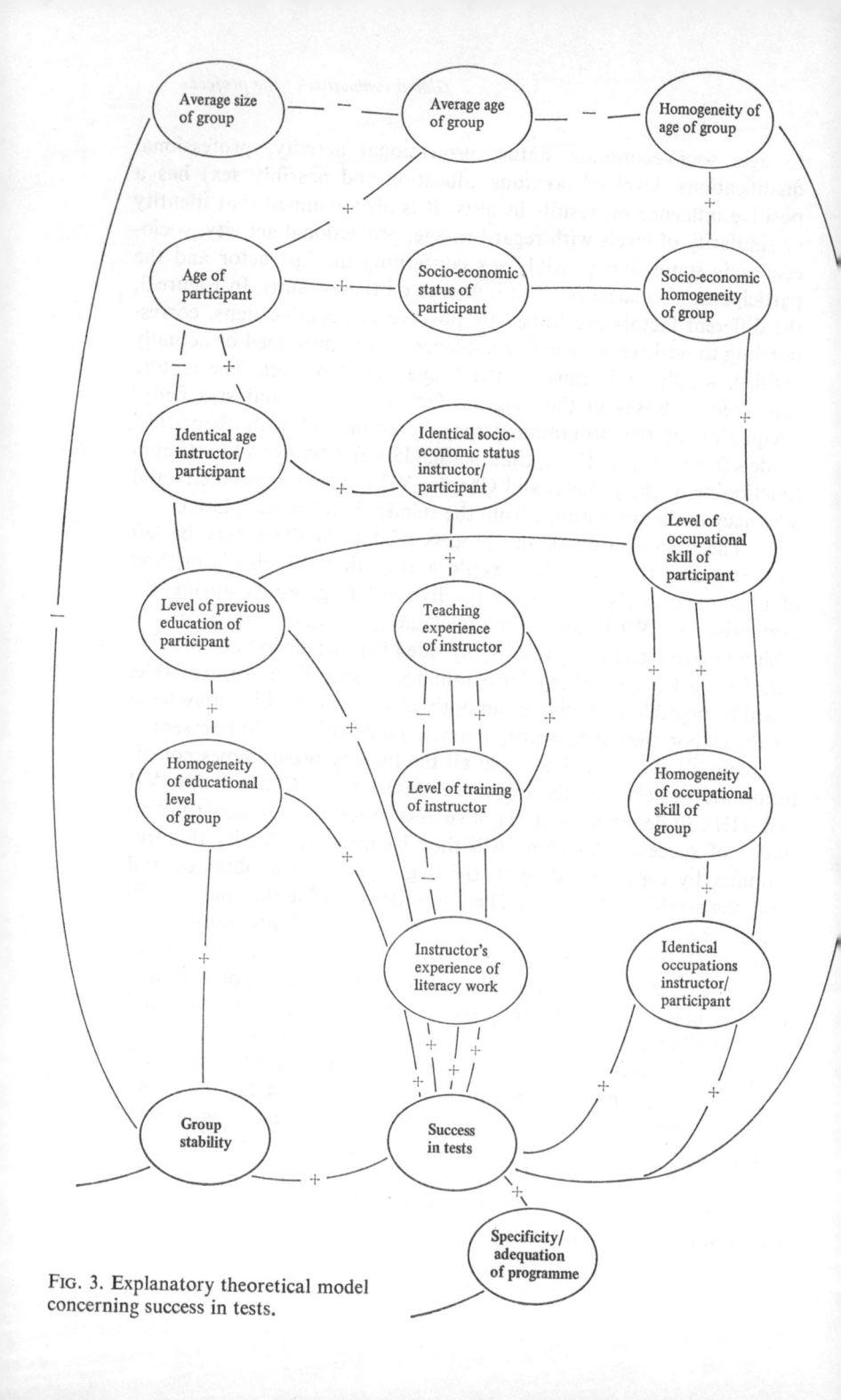

Fig. 3. Explanatory theoretical model concerning success in tests.

The characteristics which are likely to ensure success for participants.
The characteristics of instructors, and the training they should receive, to ensure that they obtain the best results.
The characteristics likely to ensure that groups obtain the greatest number of successes.
The organizational elements of the project, incorporation of which as a matter of priority is likely to ensure the greatest benefits from the resources engaged.
The programme contents, learning methods, teaching materials, etc., which are best suited to the population concerned and which should produce maximum results for the least effort on the part of the population.

We should, however, reiterate two words of caution. The first concerns evaluation in general and is related to the degree of certainty that may be accorded to conclusions (cf. Chapter II, Section 1); the second is related to the instrument selected for the measurement of results, i.e. the test, and its reliability (cf. Chapter, Section 3).

Finally, it should be pointed out that with the global evaluation of the project, we reach a critical stage in the system (see below, Fig. 6) selected for the global evaluation of EWLP. The global evaluation model provides for three frameworks of analysis: functional literacy (the independent variable); socio-economic and cultural consequences (the dependent variable); and the conditions for educational success (the intermediate variable), which are examined in the present chapter. Within each of these frameworks, the evaluator will endeavour to produce a descriptive summary of the table of variables used, to suggest different hypotheses the verification of which will permit confirmation or invalidation of assumptions concerning links between different inputs, and finally to present a series of assorted analyses which will make it possible to pass from one framework to another.

The explanatory theoretical model proposed above (Fig. 3) permits transition from the intermediate variable (educational success) to the dependent variable (socio-economic and cultural consequences) studied in Chapter VIII. The transition from the independent variable (functional literacy) to the intermediate variable is studied in Chapter VII. Figure 3 merely indicates, with the box 'specificity/adequation of programme', the point where it is inserted.

3 Evaluation of the impact of logistic components of the project

On the basis of the different factors and hypotheses described above, it might be interesting to test the following hypothetical model:

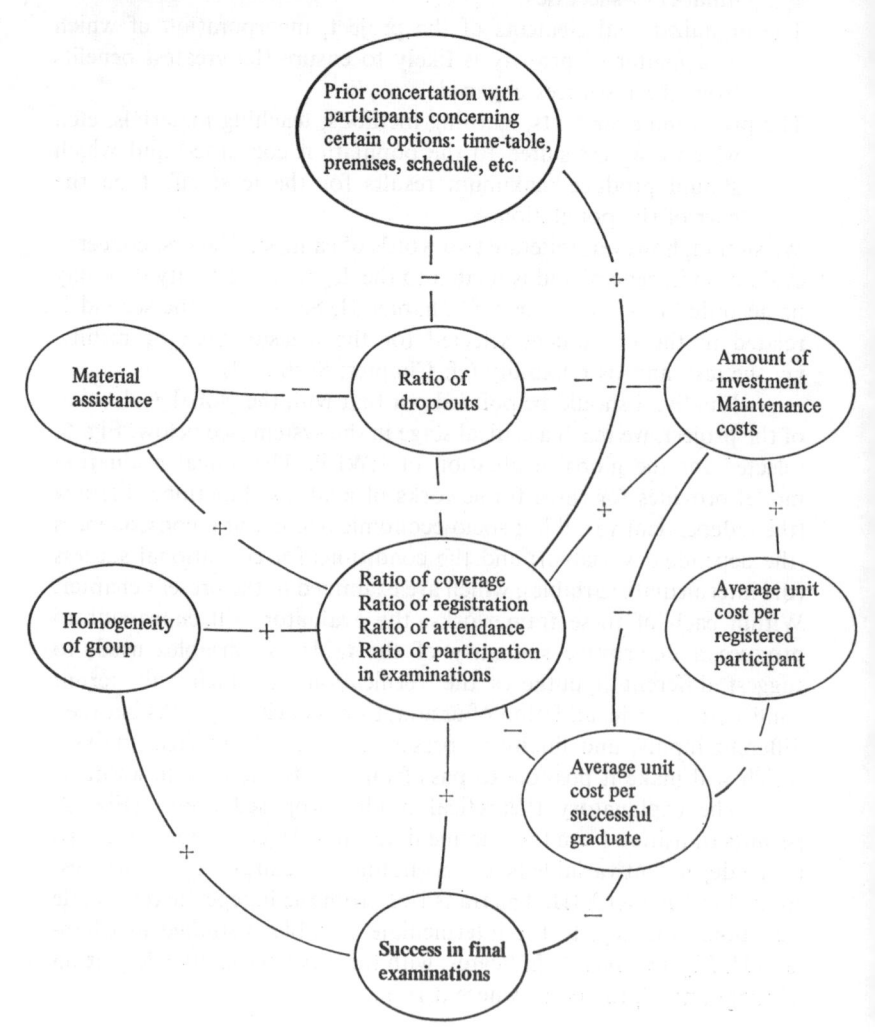

FIG. 4. Explanatory theoretical model of logistic components of the project.

Material assistance is provided (in the form of food, work time, etc.); concertation with participants is exemplary with regard to the choice of premises, time-table, etc.; the programme is adequately financed; rates of attendance, participation in tests and success in examinations are high and increasing progressively with growth of the quoted inputs. It is further assumed that the greater the allocations to investment and maintenance, i.e. the higher the average unit cost of the project per participant, the lower the average unit cost per successful participant, provided that sufficient logistic support is provided to induce higher rates of participation.

4 Evaluation of programme content

The various hypotheses described in Chapter VII may be assembled in an explanatory theoretical model of the type set out in Figure 5. This model is based on the assumption that when the major principles of functional literacy ('strategic': adequacy with regard to objectives, selectivity and specificity; and 'pedagogic': integration, inclusiveness, adaptation of materials and methods) are applied with care, quantitative returns from the system are higher, its application and progression are more satisfactory, and its qualitative returns, as measured by the results obtained in tests, are weightier.

5 Global evaluation of the project

We have just briefly indicated how it is possible, with regard to each of the main fields covered by evaluation, to unite all the relevant hypotheses in a single explanatory theoretical model.

The advantage of such models is that correlation of the different variables permits a global response to the question: what are the optimum conditions, as far as quantitative and qualitative results, profitability, logistic support and programme adequacy are concerned, for ensuring the success of a functional literacy programme?

The team responsible for the global evaluation of EWLP constructed a conceptual diagram of the functional literacy process which indicates its most important aspects and interrelations. This outline is reflected in Figure 6, while a detailed explanation will be found in the methodological introduction to Document VI of the global evaluation of EWLP, to which reference has already been made. A brief description in the words of tis author, Pierre Clément, reads:

The evaluation of literacy programmes

The framework outlines the progression from (a) the political determination to mould the adult, illiterate work-force functionally with a view to effecting the economic and psycho-cultural transformation of the milieu as the potential generator of economic and social development ... to (b) the transformation itself, through a series of measures which are socially and

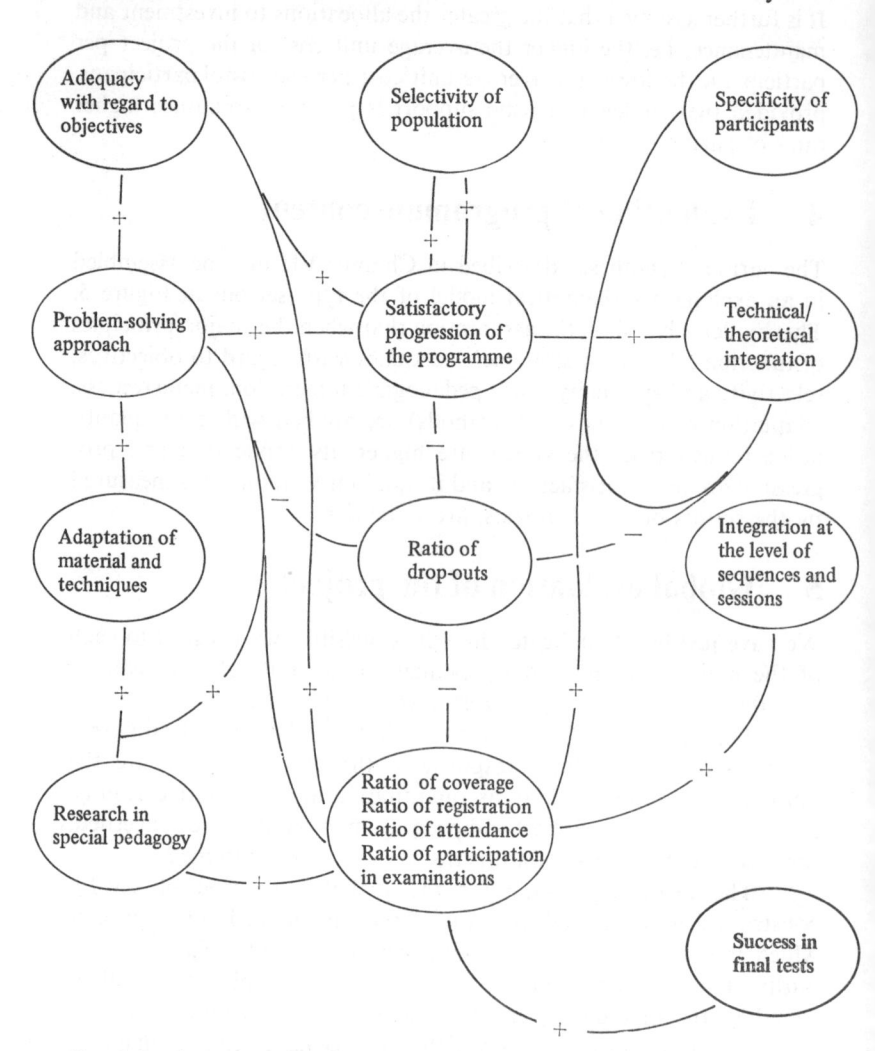

Fig. 5. Explanatory theoretical model relating to the principles of functional literacy.

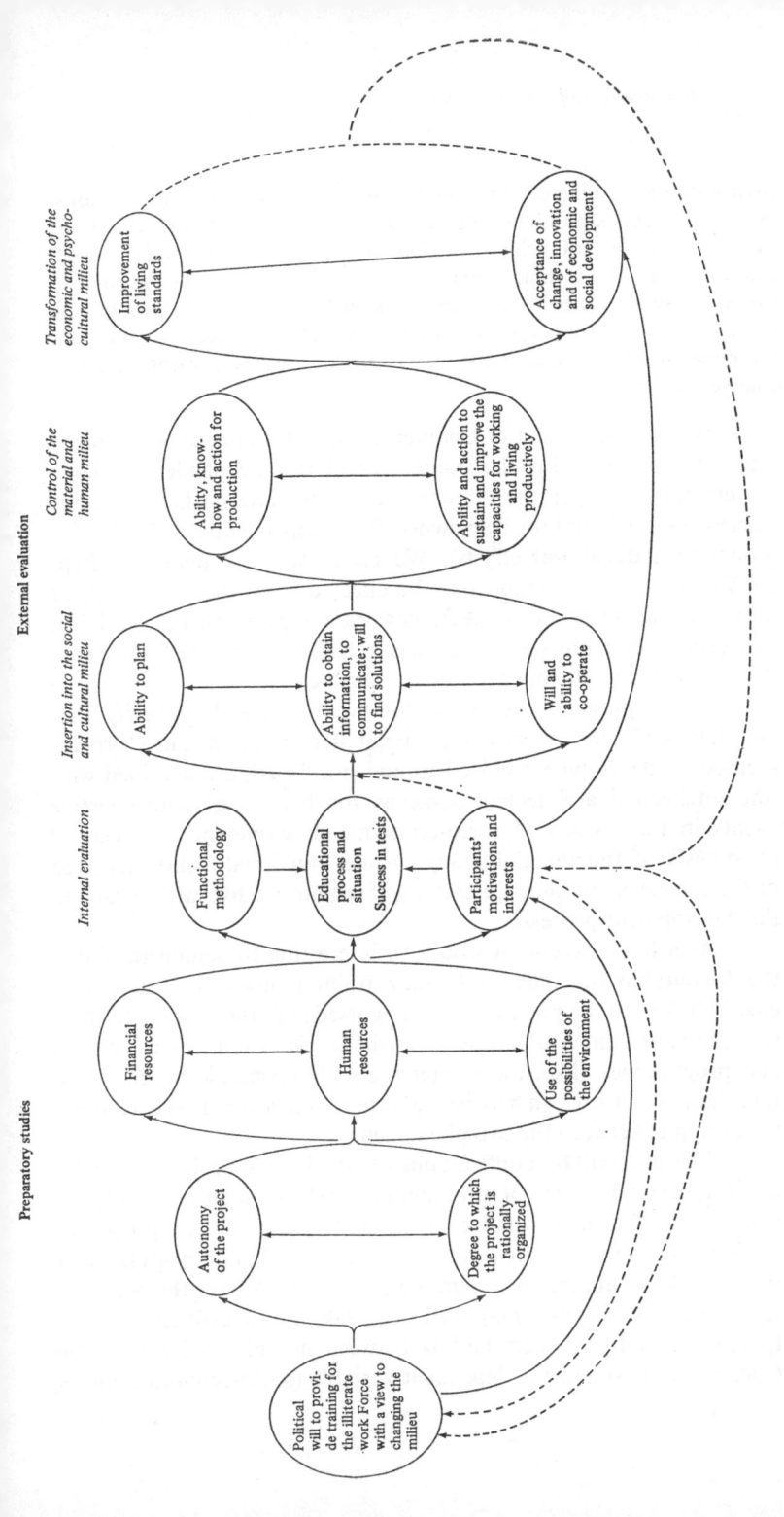

FIG. 6. Conceptual diagram of the functional literacy process.

environmentally adapted to the awareness, perceptions, motivations, interests, values, aspirations, etc. of the actors; to pedagogical action; to the broadening of fields of vision and of interest; to wider social, cultural, economic, technical and scientific horizons of knowledge; and to the expression of newly won aptitudes and opportunities through the specific actions which constitute an ultimate bridge between the conditions for material and attitudinal change favourable to development, and that change itself.

We have seen (end of Chapter V) that this outline is organized into three frameworks: the framework of the independent variable (functional literacy); the framework of the intermediate variable (success in tests); and the framework of the dependent variable (socio-economic and cultural effects). We have also seen (end of Chapter VII) how the transition may be effected from the framework of the independent variable to the framework of the intermediate variable. The general diagram shows how the transition may be effected from the intermediate to the dependent variable.

The hypotheses set out above were designed to verify that individuals who have received functional literacy training, in a 'process focused on development objectives and problems', are provided with 'the intellectual and technical means for becoming more effective agents in the process of socio-economic development' (the central hypothesis of functional literacy), while individuals who, deprived of these means, continue illiterate, will remain passive with regard to the development process.

As a final exercise, it would be interesting to demonstrate that the favourable outcome of literacy training noted above is very closely linked to the process of training itself; in other words, to show that the better the results of tests, at the levels of individuals, groups and programmes alike, the greater the socio-economic benefits; and that there is a link which may be measured (by a correlation coefficient, for example) between the two phenomena.

This task will be a difficult one for small-scale projects involving an insufficient number of programmes and commanding resources —in terms of technical and evaluation staff and of data-processing equipment—which are too limited. On the other hand, projects which involve a large number of programmes and which have the necessary means at their disposal may well undertake an investigation of this type, as a result of which the link between the intermediate variable (success in tests) and the dependent variable (socio-economic effects) may be demonstrated, and the central hypothesis of functional literacy verified, with reference to any given project.[1]

---

1. In the exercise in global evaluation of EWLP (see Select Bibliography, Document VI), which employed 167 inidcators retained after methodological processing for the evaluation of some 30 functional literacy programmes in 6 countries, it was found that a high mark (78 per cent) 'could be attributed to a global hypothesis—implicit in the central hypothesis of functional literacy—to be formulated with regard to the overall external effectiveness of such literacy training'. The document cited, with Document IV, contains all the necessary information concerning the organization of such a study, together with a description of the methodological precautions which should be observed.

Appendix

Document 1. Register of participants

Province: ....
District: ....
Town: ....
Group: ....

Year: .... Month: ....

Instructor: ....
Supervisor: ....

Number of participants originally registered in the batch ...., including .... women
Number of additions:
Total registrations at the end of the month ...., including .... women

1	2	3	4	5	6			7		
					Men			Women		
Name and first name	Sex	Age	Marital Status	Days	Aged 15-24	Aged 25-45	Aged 45+	Aged 15-24	Aged 25-45	Aged 45+
					Number of absences					
				Absences						

8
a) Number of sessions during the month:
b) Number of participants registered at the beginning of the month:
c) Number of possible attendances a) X b) :

d) Total absences:

e) Ratio of absenteeism $\frac{d}{c}$ X 100 .... %

Appendix

Document 2. Monthly report

Province and district: Year: Instructor:
                                Month: Supervisor:
Locality: Group No.:

A. Statistics

(a) Number of sessions planned, held:
(b) Number of registrations in the batch:
      Number of additional registrations:
      Number of registrations at the end of the month:
(c) Number of absences by sex and age:

Men			Women			
15/24	25/45	+ 45	15/24	25/45	+ 45	Total

(d) Number of absences by cause [1]

W	H	T	F	D	C	N	.	.	.	Total

B. Visits by supervisor

During the month (dates):
Total number of visits since the beginning of the courses:

C. Teaching material received

Individual (type and quantity) :
Collective (type and quantity) :
For instructor's use (type and quantity) :
Audio-visual (type and quantity) :

---

1. Cause-of-absence code: W = work; H = health; T = travel, emigration, seasonal migration; F = traditional holidays or festivals; D = domestic reasons, children, etc.; C = climate, bad weather; N = unidentified; etc.

Appendix

D. Assistance received

Foodstuffs (quantity):
Overtime:
Working hours:
Fertilizers, pesticides, seeds, plants, etc.:
Other:

E. Budget

(a) Salaries:
(b) Bills settled (maintenance, heating, electricity, cleaning materials, etc.):

F. Instructor's report

Indicate, for each element of the programme:
    Number of sessions planned and actually held:
    Number of sequences taught, and their serial numbers:
    Serial numbers of untaught sequences:
    Reading:
    Vocational instruction:
    Socio-economic instruction:
    General instruction:
    Other instruction:

Observations:

G. Results of weekly tests

Week 1

Subject	Number of participants tested	Critical score	Number or percentage of successful participants	Average score
Reading				
Writing				
Elementary arithmetic				
Applied arithmetic				
Etc.				

Week 2
Etc.

Appendix

Document 3. End-of-cycle report

Province and district: Year: Instructor:
    Cycle: Supervisor:
Locality: Length of cycle: Group No.:

A. Statistics

Date of first course: Date of final course:
Batch: Men: Women: Total:
Additional registrations: Men: Women: Total:
Percentage of wastage: Men: Women: Total:

B. Degree of literacy

	0-1-2	3-4	5-6
	Illiterates	Semi-literates	Literates
At beginning of batch			
At beginning of this cycle			
At conclusion of this cycle			
Course attainment (indicate + or −)			
Percentage of batch at conclusion of cycle			

C. Results of end-of-cycle examination

Tests	Number of items	Critical score	Average score obtained	Number of participants	Number and percentage of successful participants

Appendix

Document 4. Test of know-how (cotton programme)

1. How many days after the first bolls open is the cotton harvested?
2. Where are the bolls sorted?
3. Where is the cotton harvest stored?
4. Why should stalks and leaves be burnt after the harvest?
5. Is land which is suitable for growing millet also suitable for cotton?
6. Is it necessary, useful or unimportant to include cotton in a crop rotation?
7. When is early hoeing necessary?
8. Should millet and cotton be sown at the same time?
9. How many kilograms of cotton seed are required for one hectare?
10. How much space should be left between the rows?
11. How much space should be left between the seed holes?
12. How many seeds should be sown in each seed hole?
13. How many plants should be left when thinning out?
14. When is deep ploughing carried out?
15. At what time of the year does early sowing take place?
16. At what time of the year does late sowing take place?
17. At what time of the year does thinning out take place?
18. How long after sowing does the first weeding take place?
19. How long after the first weeding does the second take place?
20. How many days after sowing should fertilizer be spread?
21. How much fertilizer should be spread per hectare?
22. When should the plants be earthed up?
23. Should the plants be cut or uprooted after harvesting?
24. Should early sowing be done on level ground or on ridges?
25. What operation may be carried out at the same time as the first weeding?
26. What operation may be carried out at the same time as the second weeding?
27. What is the minimum number of treatments with insecticides?
28. How long after sowing should the first treatment take place?
29. How much time should be left between subsequent treatments?
30. How many tins of insecticide are required to prepare half a drum of mixture for the first treatment?

Appendix

Document 5. Literacy scale

Code:
Village:
Name and first name:
Age:

No.:
Has attended school for ___ years
Has attended literacy course for ___ years

Grade I

1. Holds pencil
2. Copies simple figures
3. Tells the time
4. Writes figures 1-9

Grade II

5. Carries out single figure additions and substractions
6. Writes own name
7. Reads letters
8. Writes figures in tens

Grade III

9. Adds, subtracts and multiplies in double figures
10. Writes letters
11. Reads common words
12. Writes numbers in hundreds

Grade IV

13. Recognizes triangle, rectangle and diameter
14. Writes words phonetically
15. Reads simple words
16. Writes figures in tens of thousands

Grade V

17. Carries out the four basic arithmetical operations
18. Writes simple phrases
19. Reads simple phrases word by word
20. Writes all numbers

Grade VI

21. Recognizes geometrical lines and figures
22. Composes a text
23. Reads fluently
24. Writes units of the metric system

Total = ___ = Grade

Is the pupil eager to learn?

Why?
When?

Place

Date

19

Name and signature of examiner

Appendix

Document 6. Course sheet

Province, district: Instructor:
　　　　　　　　　Supervisor:
Locality:　　　　　Group No.:

A. Premises

Premises:
State of premises:
Planned duration of cycle:　　months
Opening date of cycle:　　　　　　　Closing date:
Number of weekly sessions:
Average length of session:
Planned time-table of sessions:

B. Name of development organization to which the programme is related

Firm or company of which the majority of participants are employees:
Title of programme:
Cycle:
Observations concerning the degree of homogeneity of occupations of the participants:

C. Statistics

Number of participants registered: Total:　　Men:　　Women

	Years of age				
	Less than 15	15/24	25/34	35/44	45 +

Men
Women
Married
Possessing a common
occupational characteristic

D. Before the course opened

Had the instructor received vocational training?
Had the instructor received in-service training (state dates, duration, level)?
Was the teaching material for pupils ready?

E. Does a literacy committee exist? Composition?

Is specialist assistance provided for the course? (By whom? When?)

Appendix

Type, nature and quantity of assistance provided by the development organization?

F. Course material (type and quantity)

Furniture:
Teaching material:
  For the instructor's use:
  For individual use by participants:
  For collective use by participants:
  Audio-visual:

G. Feeding and maintenance of participants

Include information concerning lighting, heating, cleaning of premises, transport, etc.

H. Expenditure by the centre

J. Aid received

Materials, fertilizers, pesticides, etc.
Extra hours, working hours surrendered, etc.

K. Difficulties encountered

Appendix

Document 7. Dimensions, criteria and indicators for the evaluation of social, economic and psycho-cultural changes

(for a programme of functional literacy training for mine workers)

List of tables which might be prepared on the basis of data provided by measurement of the selected indicators.

Dimension 1: The will to change

Criterion 1: Importance and variety of motivations

1.1.1. Number of expressions of the wish to learn the basic techniques of literacy—reading, writing, etc.—sex, age group, socio-economic status, etc. (the listing might correspond to the main characteristics of the participants).
1.1.2. Number of requests for teaching in subjects related to participants' occupation or to the firm for which they work, listed according to the selected characteristics.
1.1.3. Number of requests for intellectual teaching in matters related to the exercise of the participant's occupation.
1.1.4. Number of requests for teaching in technical subjects directly related to the participant's job.
1.1.5. Number of requests for teaching in subjects related to the maintenance and improvement of the participant's productive energies.
1.1.6. Number of requests for teaching in subjects related to participants' relations with their environment (geographical, physical, economic, social, political, etc.).

Criterion 2: Objectives, ambitions

1.2.1. List of advantages which participants expect to gain from literacy training.
1.2.2. List of environmental factors which, in the opinion of participants, may hamper their efforts to become literate.
1.2.3. List of motives for a desire for a change of situation (job, trade, employer, locality, country), and if appropriate the causes.

Dimension 2: Learning

See sections 1 and 2, Chapter IX, on the quantitative and qualitative evaluation of results.

Dimension 3: Ability to plan, to organize and to solve problems

Criterion 1: Scholarization of children

3.1.1. Number of children attending school compared with the number of children of school age of the families concerned.
3.1.2. Number of children of school age who have abandoned their studies.
3.1.3. Ratios of scholarization and of drop-outs in the localities where literacy teaching is being provided.

Appendix

Criterion 2: Family budgeting

3.2.1. Number of households keeping accounts.
3.2.2. Day-to-day expenditure on food, health and medicine, leisure activities, obligations, etc.
3.2.3. Amount of savings and manner of saving (bank or other deposits, not deposited).
3.2.4. Amount of loans accorded and manner of lending (modern or traditional).
3.2.5. Amount of borrowings and manner of borrowing (modern or traditional: usury); reasons for borrowing.
3.2.6. Volume (or quantity) of reserves and stocks, by type (goods for family consumption, seed grains, goods for repayment, fertilizers, pesticides, medicines, etc.).
3.2.7. Estimated value of the estate and volume of productive investment: land, buildings, furniture, vehicles, machinery, tools and implements, livestock, etc.
3.2.8. Volume or list of non-productive but utilitarian goods and equipment: clothes, household articles, etc.
3.2.9. List of non-productive and non-utilitarian goods (i.e. belongings kept for reasons of prestige: cattle, gold, etc.).

Criterion 3: Family planning

3.3.1. Number of children by family and by maternal age group.
3.3.2. Number of children born during each three-year period following marriage.
3.3.3. Number of couples practising contraception.
3.3.4. Number of couples who consider that the ideal family should contain one, two, three or more children, by number of children.

Dimension 4: Will to obtain and impart information

Criterion 1: Utilization of mass media

4.1.1. Number of daily, weekly and monthly newspapers and magazines purchased and/or read, by statistical unit (individual, family, community) and by unit of time.
4.1.2. Number of radio and television sets owned and in use.
4.1.3. Amount of time spent listening to or viewing programmes, by unit of time and type of programme (news, specialized programmes, music, etc.).
4.1.4. Number of tape-recorders and cassettes, and amount of time spent listening, by unit of time and type of content.

Criterion 2: Recourse to other sources of information and to appropriate sources of assistance

By statistical unit and unit of time

4.2.1. Number of requests for advice addressed to professional organizations (trade unions, etc.) or to civic or administrative bodies (municipal authorities, village councils, etc.).

Appendix

4.2.2. Number of requests for advice addressed to welfare services (social security, mutual aid, insurance, etc.).
4.2.3. Number of requests for advice addressed to family-planning counsellors.
4.2.4. Number of requests for advice addressed to cultural centres or religious and doctrinal bodies.
4.2.5. Number of requests for advice addressed to banks, credit unions, etc.
4.2.6. Number of journeys undertaken, by duration, distance and type: family reasons, seasonal migration, search for employment, religious grounds, etc.

Criterion 3: Social and informative utilization of reading and writing
By statistical unit and unit of time
4.3.1. Number of written communications received or sent, by type: personal or administrative correspondence, exchange of information, miscellaneous.
4.3.2. Number of official forms filled out, by type: administrative, professional, postal services, co-operative, etc.
4.3.3. Number of diaries, notebooks, almanacs, yearbooks, etc., utilized.

Dimension 5: Participation

Each of the organizations listed below should be the subject of a table indicating the degree and intensity of participation by workers receiving literacy training (experimental sample) and by workers not receiving literacy training (control sample), with information concerning: membership, office-holding, attendance and involvement, speech-making, etc.

Criterion 1: Economic organizations

5.1.1. Trade unions.
5.1.2. Co-operatives.
5.1.3. Joint management-worker bodies.

Criterion 2: Social organizations

5.2.1. Traditional assemblies.
5.2.2. Cultural and religious organizations.
5.2.3. Mutual aid societies.
5.2.4. Sports associations.

Criterion 3: Political and civic organizations

5.3.1. Community administration.
5.3.2. Political parties.
5.3.3. Groups of notables, judges, local 'wise men'.
5.3.4. Regional or national delegations.

Dimension 6: Know-how and action (at the productive level)

Criterion 1: Vocational skills

6.1.1. Level of qualification in the principal and (if any) secondary occupation: technician, skilled worker, semi-skilled, unskilled, labourer, casual worker, etc.

Appendix

6.1.2. Main job description according to mental or intellectual capacities required (e.g. reasoning, speed of comprehension, memory, imagination, initiative, observation, concentration, visual alertness, manual dexterity, tenacity, artistic sense, etc.).
6.1.3. Performance rating.
6.1.4. Output (quantity, by unit of time) in the principal occupation.
6.1.5. Quality of output in the principal occupation.
6.1.6. Length of employment: in present job; with present employer; in present occupation; in present locality.
6.1.7. Degree of wasted capacity in present job.

Criterion 3: Work habits

6.2.1. Absenteeism: by unit of time (monthly, quarterly, annual) and by cause.
6.2.2. Punctuality: late arrivals over given period.
6.2.3. Observance of safety precautions: wearing of helmets, goggles, gloves and other protective clothing; observance of smoking prohibition, use of safety mechanisms, etc.: number of breaches of regulations by type and by period.
6.2.4. Number and gravity of accidents by period: type of accident and number of days lost.
6.2.5. Maintenance of machinery and tools: observance of standard regulations, frequency of greasing, etc. Number and duration of breakdowns by period.
6.2.6. Care of working environment: cleanliness, scouring, observance of regulations, etc., by period.

Criterion 3: In-service training

6.3.1. Number of courses followed: frequency, duration, level, by age, seniority, grade.
6.3.2. Pre-employment training: duration, by sex, age, grade.
6.3.3. Nature and duration of in-service apprenticeship.

Dimension 7: Know-how and action (conservation and reproduction of manpower)

Criterion 1: Health habits

7.1.1. Number of medical and pre-natal consultations by unit of time.
7.1.2. Number of births attended by doctors or qualified midwives.
7.1.3. Number of infant deaths: between birth and 1 year, 1-3 years old, more than 3 years old — by unit of time.
7.1.4. Number of preventive measures, per month and type of measure.
7.1.5. Number of families maintaining medicine chests.

Criterion 2: Hygiene

7.2.1. Number of hygienic practices by unit of time: baths, showers, dental care, etc.

Criterion 3: Nutrition

7.3.1. Structure of diet: main ingredients and frequency of meals.

Appendix

7.3.2. Hygienic practices with regard to foodstuffs: boiling water or milk, filtering water, protecting foodstuffs from insects, dust, etc.

Dimension 8: Higher living standards (economic dimension)

Criterion 1: Factors and volume of production

(See 6.1.4. and 6.1.5. for handicraft or industrial output.)
Agricultural production (principal or secondary occupation).

8.1.1. Area cultivated (or number of coffee plants, cacao trees, fruit trees, etc.) by crop.
8.1.2. Non-cultivated areas by type (fallow land, pasture, forest, scrub, marshland, etc.).
8.1.3. Main crop production (in weight or volume): quantity harvested, marketed, consumed, stored (seed), by crop.
8.1.4. Livestock: number on the hoof, marketed, consumed, by type of animal.
8.1.5. Small animals: number on the hoof, marketed, consumed, by type of animal.
8.1.6. Ancillary production: hunting, fishing, gathering, vegetable gardening, bee-keeping, etc.

Criterion 2: Family budget

8.2.1. Basic income of each member of the family.
8.2.2. Additional income (secondary occupations).
8.2.3. Allowances, bonuses, etc.
8.2.4. Value of production marketed, by product.

Criterion 3: Consumption of durable goods

8.3.1. Expenditure on the functional improvement of living accommodation and storage space, by type, cost and/or number of man-hours involved: e.g. construction of roofs, windows, kitchen, installation of running water, showers, lighting, ventilation, etc.
8.3.2. Means of production (ploughs, carts, seed drills, etc.) by type.
8.3.3. Goods and equipment: see 3.2.7.-3.2.9.
8.3.4. Number of families possessing durable goods which contribute to improved living standards, e.g. bicycles, alarm clocks and watches, radio and television sets.
8.3.5. Number of households possessing some elements of comfort, e.g. running water, lighting, electricity or gas, baths or showers, lavatories, etc.

Dimension 9: Higher living standards (psycho-cultural dimension)

9.1.1. Opinions concerning women: number of persons in favour of monogamy, literacy, education and wage-earning employment for women, female participation in the administration of local affairs, etc.
9.1.2. Degree of ambition with regard to the future of offspring.
Etc.

Appendix

Document 8. List of hypotheses formulated for the global evaluation of EWLP

Hypotheses for internal evaluation

Hypotheses concerning the characteristics of participants

1. The results of functional literacy action vary according to the degree of homogeneity of the groups of participants in terms of age, sex, activity and occupational status.
2. Age, marital status, family situation, degree of literacy prior to functional literacy training, and social and economic status all affect: registration; attendance; attrition; participation in examinations; success in examinations; retention of knowledge; adoption of practices recommended during the programmes; attitudinal and behavioural changes.
3. The effectiveness of functional literacy training depends on the participant/instructor ratio applied in the programmes.

Hypotheses concerning the characteristics and training of instructors

4. The performances of participants are affected by certain characteristics of their instructors: age, level of previous training, professional experience, familiarity with the application of literacy training methods; more particularly, instructors whose occupations and socio-economic status are identical with those of participants obtain better results than professional teachers and instructors whose occupations and socio-economic status are different.
5. A short but intensive period of initial training followed by periodic refresher courses constitutes a more effective technique for the training of instructors than a lengthy initial course without refresher training.
6. The extent to which the training of instructors is practical and centred on the basic principles and rules for the utilization of teaching material has a direct bearing on the effectiveness of such training.
7. The effectiveness of functional literacy training depends on the extent to which the instructional programme can be improved in the light of acquired experience, changing conditions and feedback from practical experience.

Hypotheses concerning the methods and means of functional literacy training

8. Training in functional literacy leads to positive changes, on

Appendix

condition that it is linked with an authentic process of political, social or technical innovation of concern to the participants.

9. The effectiveness of a functional literacy programme is related to the degree of specificity with which development objectives and the associated objectives of training are defined.
10. The more programmes are centred on problems actually encountered by participants in the course of their work, the greater the effectiveness of functional literacy training.
11. The more fully the content and material of programmes take account of the cultural environment of the participants and are presented in a language which is familiar to the latter, the greater the effectiveness of functional literacy training.
12. Integration of the content of programmes increases the effectiveness of functional literacy training.
13. The effectiveness of functional literacy training depends on an optimum relationship between the intensity of the teaching/learning process (measured by the frequency of courses) and its duration.
14. The effectiveness of the teaching material employed depends on the extent to which its different elements are integrated and programmed.

Hypotheses for external evaluation

Hypotheses concerning adaptation to the milieu

15. Functional literacy encourages the integration of individuals with their social and cultural milieu by encouraging them to extend the temporal framework of their activities and to adopt more rational patterns of behaviour resulting in a greater degree of autonomy in the quest for solutions to their problems and in the pursuit of learning, for themselves and for their offspring, thus consolidating their social adaptation.
16. Functional literacy encourages the development of improved forward-looking attitudes (prospective dimension).
17. The rate of scholarization of children of adults receiving functional literacy training is significantly higher than the rate observed among children from illiterate families.
18. Adults who have received functional literacy training frequently manifest more foresighted attitudes with regard to savings, family planning, etc. than illiterates.

Appendix

19. Functional literacy encourages the development of attitudes leading to the autonomous acquisition of objectively useful knowledge (self-training) (cognito/acquisitive dimension).
20. Adults who have received functional literacy training express more than illiterates a clear preference for radio broadcasts dealing with agricultural and/or educational subjects.
21. Adults who have received functional literacy training are more inclined than illiterates to seek opinions, advice and technical assistance from competent organizations or individuals.
22. Functional literacy encourages the development of community solidarity and associative behaviour (integrational dimension).
23. Adults who have received functional literacy training are more inclined than illiterates to set everyday problems and their solution against the background of the community.
24. Adults who have received functional literacy training tend more actively than illiterates to participate in collective organizations (professional, cultural, religious or recreational associations, etc.).

Hypotheses concerning control of the milieu

25. Functional literacy training encourages participants to control their human and material environment through the development of their practical knowledge and the adoption of more rational procedures in productive activities and in the protection of health.
26. Adults who have received functional literacy training have a more positive attitude to their work, possess greater technical knowledge and apply this knowledge more thoroughly, than illiterates.
27. There is less absenteeism among functionally literate workers than among illiterates.
28. The performance of workers who have received functional literacy training is appreciably more highly rated by their superiors (engineers, technicians, foremen) than that of illiterates.
29. Familiarity and understanding with regard to technical and productive practices (concerning technical standards and the means and inputs of production) are greater among adults who have received functional literacy training than among illiterates.
30. The adoption of technical and productive practices (involving technical standards and modern inputs) and/or up-to-date

technical and economic standards is more pronounced among adults who have received functional literacy training than among illiterates exposed to factors external to the project.

31. The adoption of more rational technical and productive standards (with regard to agricultural time-tables, methods of cultivation, working procedures, etc.) is more prevalent among adults who have received functional literacy training than among illiterates.

32. The adoption of modern inputs (pesticides, fertilizers, high-yield seeds, etc.) is more prevalent among producers who have received functional literacy training than among illiterates.

33. Participants in functional literacy programmes are more familiar than illiterates with modern techniques for the preservation and reproduction of human capacities and energies (practices related to health, hygiene and nutrition), and adopt these techniques more consistently.

Hypotheses concerning the transformation of the milieu

34. Functional literacy training encourages participants to transform their economic and psycho-cultural environment by aiding them to give practical effect to the intellectual, social and economic potential they have acquired, by inciting them to improve their living standards and by generating attitudes favourable to innovation and development.

35. Participants in functional literacy programmes produce, earn and consume more than illiterates (economic dimension).

36. Means of production and output (in terms of substance and/or value) increase faster among participants in functional literacy programmes than among non-participants living under comparable conditions.

37. Real or potential monetary income and/or property are greater among participants in functional literacy programmes than among non-participants.

38. Consumption of durable goods is higher among adults who have received functional literacy training than among illiterates.

39. To a greater extent than illiterates, adults who have received functional literacy training are amenable to economic and social progress, are aware of the ways and means of achieving such progress and of their own role in the process, are inclined to adopt rational approaches to the solution of problems and are

Appendix

concerned with the quality and value of their work (psycho-cultural dimension).
40. Adults who have received functional literacy training are more inclined than illiterates to reject values and structures which impede development and to look in the direction of change and innovation.
41. Participants in functional literacy programmes are more favourable than illiterates to economic planning and calculation.
42. Functional literacy training renders individuals more aware of their responsibility for the improvement of the well-being of the community and better disposed to assume that responsibility.
43. Functional literacy training develops awareness of the material and moral benefits that adult education can bring both to individuals and to the community.
44. Confidence in modern technological achievements and understanding of the origins of natural phenomena are more pronounced among adults who have received functional literacy training than among illiterates.
45. Adults who have received functional literacy training are less concerned than illiterates with the purely material aspect of their work, and are more concerned with quality of performance.
46. The desire for promotion and for occupational mobility within and beyond their present employment is stronger among adults who have received functional literacy training than among illiterates.

The above hypotheses are taken from the documentation of the global evaluation of EWLP (Document VII for internal, and Document VI for external, evaluation). Needless to say, other hypotheses may be formulated in these two fields and others, more particularly in respect of action taken prior to the launching of a functional literacy project and to the definition of its institutional framework: insertion of the project into the political context; determination of degree of autonomy of the project; integration with national institutions; internal organization of the project; assessment of the material and human resources at its disposal, etc.

Select bibliography

Global Evaluation of EWLP, Technical Documents, Unesco, 1975:[1]

Document I: Le Concept d'Alphabétisation Fonctionnelle: Genèse, Objectifs et Hypothèses du PEMA.
Document II: Le Cadre Institutionnel des Projets Expérimentaux.
Document III: La Méthodologie de l'Alphabétisation Fonctionnelle.
Document IV: Evaluation Méthodologique du Cadre Expérimental.
Document V: Alphabétisation Fonctionnelle et Apprentissage: l'Évaluation du Processus d'Enseignement-Apprentissage.
Document VI: Alphabétisation Fonctionnelle et Développement: Les Effets Économiques et Sociaux du Processus d'Enseignement-Apprentissage.
Document VII: Mise en Relation des Modalités de l'Action Pédagogique et des Effets Socio-économiques de l'Alphabétisation Fonctionnelle.
Document VIII: (In preparation.)
Document IX: Coûts et Rendements de l'Alphabétisation Fonctionnelle.

Manuel pour l'Évaluation des Projets d'Alphabétisation Fonctionnelle, Unesco, 1970. (In French only.)

Practical Guide to Functional Literacy, Unesco, 1973.

The Training of Functional Literacy Personnel—A Practical Guide, Unesco, 1973.

Work-oriented Adult Literacy Pilot Project—Iran, Final Technical Report, 9 vol., 1975.

1. These technical documents (in French only) have not yet been published, but may be consulted at Unesco Headquarters in Paris, in the Documentation Unit of the Literacy, Adult Education and Rural Development Division (ED/LAR).

Index

Absenteeism, 79-81
Adequacy of programmes, 105, 113
Aid (material), 116-17
Aims of projects, 61-2
Analyses, 57
Attendance at courses, 77, 80
Autonomy of project, 64, 90

Baseline surveys, 27, 29, 46, 66, 71
Budgets. *See* Finance

Change (socio-economic), 30, 48, 120, 155
Comparative studies, 57, 79, 88, 124
Components of programme, 78, 114
Contents of programme, 29, 67, 103
Control (statistical), 33
Courses (organization), 96, 100

Definitions (objectives), 32, 61
Descriptive studies, 57, 66, 78, 87, 98, 124
Development of programme, 105, 113
Discussions with authorities, 39
Documents, search for, 38
Drop-out, 79, 80

Environment. *See* Milieu
Evaluation
  global, 28, 133
  internal, external, 34, 119
  limitations, 37
  sectional, 27, 61, 77, 83, 96, 103, 120
Examinations, 77
Experimental World Literacy Programme (EWLP), 26, 37, 160
Experts' judgements, 108
Explanatory studies, 38, 80, 89, 100, 112

Feasibility. *See* Studies
Feedback (intervention), 89, 124
Field visits, 40
Finance, 65, 89, 97, 101

Groups
  characteristics, 96
  experimental, 28, 44, 53
  structure, 28, 100

Homogeneity tests, 55, 124
Hypotheses,
  central, 25, 44, 58, 131
  change, 126-31

Index

EWLP, 160
 logistical. *See* Logistics
 programme, 113-20
 yield, 80, 89-94

Indicators,
 basic measurements, 43, 48, 52, 155
 of knowledge, 51
Indices, 122
Information, 46
Instructional technology, 33
Instructors, 95-7
Integration, 114, 127
Interim studies. *See* Studies

Logistics
 hypotheses, 100-103
 internal, 95
Literacy
 functional, 25-7
 scale, 85

Materials
 teaching, 107, 116
Methods
 evaluation, 38
 teaching, 107, 114
Milieu
 changes in, 130
 integration, 127
 studies, 48, 62, 64, 66, 91, 96, 105
Models, 80, 89, 98-102, 112, 126, 139
Monographs, technical, 46
Motivation surveys. *See* Studies

Observation sheets, 41

Participants
 characteristics, 77, 88, 94
Planning, 28-9, 72-5
Political will, 64, 90
Principles of functional literacy, 103-16
Problem investigation, 69
Programmes (projects)
 experimental, 28
 literacy, 68
 operational, 32
Publicity, 46

Questionnaires, 41

Resources, 65, 97
Results, 87-9

Samples, 33, 41, 55-6, 66, 125-31
Statistics
 attendance, participation registration, drop-out, 33, 48-9
 evaluation of change, 155
 logistics, 98
 programme content, 109
 success, 86
 yield, 77, 87
Studies
 feasibility, 27-8, 29, 63-6, 109-16
 final, 43, 78-80, 87-94, 123-31
 initial, 43, 61, 71
 interim, 43, 48-55
 logistics, 98-101
 motivation, 61, 65, 69-70

Tests, 33, 55, 84-5, 86, 89, 93, 122, 123

[A. 24] ED 77/D 95/A